# The Poet's Domain

# The Poet's Domain

*Collection of Poems*

**Volume Twenty-Two**

*And I Rejoiced in Being What I Was*

Compiled and edited by
Patricia S. Adler

Live Wire Press
1-866-579-3850
www.livewirepress.net

Cover art: Rose on Papyrus © by Terry Cox-Joseph

For information contact:
e-mail: padler@cstone.net
www.livewirepress.net

If you are unable to order this book from your local
bookseller, you may order directly from the publisher.
Call 1-866-579-3850 toll free.

Library of Congress Cataloging-in-Publication Data

And I Rejoiced in Being What I Was . . ./ compiled and edited by Patricia S.
Adler.
    p. cm. — (The poet's domain; v. 22)
  ISBN 0-9727531-2-5 (alk. paper)
  1. American poetry—Middle Atlantic States. 2. American poetry—20th
century. 3. Millay, Edna St. Vincent, 1895-1950. First fig—Poetry.
I. Adler, Patricia S., 1938-   . II. Series.
PS545.M9 2001
811'.6080974—dc21

                                                    2001005477
          10 9 8 7 6 5 4 3 2 1

Printed in the United States

# Dedication

To the torch bearers in this grand relay of life.

# Table of Contents

# Editor's Note

Once again, it is my great pleasure and honor to bring this work forward.

Patricia S. Adler
Publisher

## On the Crow River

In winter, the Crow was a black stroke
brushed through frozen fields past
woods of birch and pine,

unplowed county roads where
the Lutheran steeple stood
sentinel over farms

deep in muffled snow—Hannulas,
Rutsinoijas, Wodijas, whose old
folk still

kept to Finnish ways. Some said they
could whistle up the wind, get the news
from gossiping birds

and knew how the future lay
from the cast of rune-like alders on
the river's frosty banks

bare branches that December night
strung in beads of ice
that trapped the amber firelight

where we warmed and skated
holding hands, or raced, all of us

rattling hard over washboard ridges
our shouts and laughter hanging dry
and stiff

in winter cold
until
some Arctic shift changed everything

and in the oddly altered air
we linked arms, a single wing on
the icy Crow

that swept and pulled,
speeding us thru bursts of polar light
and the sizzle of cold heat singing.

*Sunday Abbott*

of Virginia Beach was born during a snowstorm in North Dakota. She rejoices in having grown up in Minnesota where, like her birthplace, winters are often six months long and cold as the back of the moon. Blizzards and sub-zero winds swept down from the Pole causing folks to draw closer for warmth, except for the children, who were thrilled with the cold magic of ice and now. The poems that appear here are remnants of that Minnesota weather.

Sunday Abbott

## Giving Thanks

They're pounding at the door    shouting hello
laughing as they tell how the blizzard iced
        windows
so they couldn't see the road
like going over the falls in a barrel someone says

coming out of the sharp freeze    brushing off snow
stamping    feet    joking in embarrassment
as they bump pulling off boots
in the intimacy of the narrow entry

hugging in the kitchen's warm wooly steam
of cooking potatoes and rutabagas
thick comforting smells of baking turkey
apples    sage    cinnamon    thyme

all of us happy    quarrels forgot
no one wasting    waning    missing
all of us present—aunts    uncles    cousins

mother basting the turkey she'd gotten up early
to singe    pluck and stuff    grandma unpacking pies
aunty whipping cream with a clattering hand-
        cranked beater

all of us lit by lamplight and candlefire    dad's
        steady voice
asking blessings    giving thanks
as icy winds scrape the old house    rattle
        windows and latch

no one thinking of risky roads    the long trip home
back then when everything hoped for was yet
        to come.

## The Cat Who Loved My Sister

Butch Van Aernum.
Star in a long line of black cats.
A lean, mean fighting machine.
Fringed ears and a missing fang
testified to his nightly forays.
Carolyn Elizabeth.
Creature magnet to people and animals alike.
Auburn hair and bright blue eyes
and a demeanor inviting to all.
Butch was most smitten.
To gain her attention and affection,
he would bring her evidence of his hunting
prowess:
mouse tails, which he carefully arranged
next to her high, four-poster cannonball bed
where she would be sure to step on them
when she got up in the morning.
She invariably reacted with a shriek of dismay
and then laughter.
Marking his territory, and ensuring her
attention,
on occasion, he would go into her closet
and poop in a shoe.
I was forever grateful that cat did not love me!

*Barbara Achilles*

(b.1931, Knowlesville, N.Y.) for-
mer music director and scriptwriter
and a retired intelligence officer.
She graduated from the Eastman
School of Music and the College
of Arts and Sciences, University of
Rochester. Her poetry has appeared
in volumes 5 through 21 of *The
Poet's Domain* and the 9th and
10th Anniversary editions of the
*Poetry Society of Virginia
Anthologies*. She is moderator of
The Poets of Tallwood Workshop
of the Osher Lifelong Learning
Institute at George Mason
University. A resident of Vienna,
Va., she is a member of the
National League of American
Pen Women.

Barbara Achilles

## Senior Trips

Another ELDERHOSTEL catalogue invites
visions of roads clogged with wily travelers
frantically scampering from dorm to dorm
ingesting a diet of information on subjects
they may only incidentally care about.
A cheap week of sightseeing and camaraderie
in some place they may not have been before.

Sharing the fears of advancing years.
Running away from home—
away from meaningless meaningful relationships
and material things.

Time-rich and free.
Relieved to discover
life was not meant to have meaning;
the incredible experience is enough.

## The Stage

Footlights glow
audience dissolves to black
spotlights warm the scene
A comforting calm descends
upon this structured world
Haven for the timid
with its carefully planned plot
tight direction
choreographed moves
dialogue and gestures
determined and timed.
Emotion controlled
to a degree.
A new identity.
No wonder I aspired
to this safe place
that brings
notice and applause.
Would that all the world
were a stage.

Barbara Achilles

## The Eighth Commandment Redux

A band of little bandits
waited in the old pew
on the porch of the general store
until a pea wagon
appeared on the bridge.

When it rounded the corner
on the road to the viner,
the raid was on.
Little bandit feet in hot pursuit.
Little bandit hands pulling
long, leafy chains from the stack,
dragging them back to the pew
where a pod-popping feast began.

The victim smiled and drove on.
He had come to expect
these daily encounters
and was happy to share his bounty
with these ragamuffins.

The viner has been closed
for many years.
It has been a long time
since anyone condoned petit larceny
or since little bandits
stole vegetables for a snack.

## Gratitude

I walk the earth
and loathe am I to leave
these stars and moon
and oceans full;
these trees and winds
and creatures large and small.
My heart is full
of what my eyes have seen
and all creation
is in my "I."

*Patricia Adler*

was born in Elizabeth, New Jersey.
Her life has revolved around the
expression of the "word"—spoken,
sung, written —in poetry and
prose, and even in art form.

## Curriculum Vitae

A falling star, a flashing minnow
Offer brilliant biographies;

Crocus and witch hazel both,
Aptly, open and close a season.

Mushroom democrats? Cheer up—
We're numbered among the stars!

*Don Amburgey*

(b.1936, Knott County, Kentucky) Don has been a teacher in one-room schools, an outdoor drama producer, and a regional library developer for the Kentucky Department of Libraries & Archives, Frankfort, Kentucky, 1961–1991. He attended UK Library School. Since retirement he has written nearly 100 poems, short stories, and songs. Some of the publishers: *Kentucky Folklore Record, Pegasus, Laurels, Modern Haiku, Potpourri*, and PSV. He combines storytelling with guitar and banjo playing at schools, libraries, and senior citizen's centers. He lives with wife, Joyce, a librarian, in Jenkins, Kentucky. They have 3 children and 5 grandchildren.

# Dancers

Just barely dusk I watch
the warm mist curtain being parted
to present the silent silver stage

wondering, if Grace descends at nightfall
awakening syncopated frog choruses
to chant the great "Aa-Uuu-Mmmm"

like brown-caped monks transformed;
using their great leaping legs
to become cosmic ballet dancers,

while twisting, dancing, singing,
still opening the universe's stored treasure
to our most ancient memory sounds.

Do these frogs with their big eyes
bother to dance above this silver stage
to see the clouds, the trees and me

or, does Grace descend to part the mist
and light the stage when my mind changes
to enlarge the things it can call beautiful?

Jason Atkins

Jason Atkins was born in
Hampton, Va. He attended
Huntington School of Engineering
and University of Oklahoma.
While in the U.S. Navy, he was a
gunner and a torpedo bomber. He
was employed 30 years by AON
Corp. and is now retired. He is
acting facilitator of Old Dominion
University's Writer's Group. He
has been published in *Holiday*
magazine, *Borders Magazine, The
Poets Domain, New England
Anthology, In Good Company,
Writers Voice, West Virginia
Review* and the *Beacon*.

Jason Atkins

# Mountain Midwife

"Orelena's" 100th Birthday Wish
(Groundhog Mountain: Floyd, Co. Va.: June 22, 1937)

Each morning I awake
on this mountain,
discovering the new sun
flashing its long rays
down into the valley,
showering diamonds
in the fog,
lighting up
a jeweled promised land,
just for me.

Some bright morning
I want to enter death,
sailing on a sunbeam,
wearing my best blue dress,
with my eyes wide open,
with my arms wide open
in welcome, ready
to hear
the voices
of my waiting children,
introducing me
to God.

## The First Time

It took us two years to complete "the act"
from the first time you put your tongue in my
mouth.

I treated my virginity like a *Weight Watchers'*
dessert—
one piece at a time, while my identity opened
wide
to swallow *Raaape!* with every crumb
(the aftertaste of all those forced-feedings as a
child).

Struggling and shaking,
I couldn't even slap my monsters on the ass—
let alone confront them face to face.

But your touch was timid with
respect, it seemed,
for that unsureness, connecting
itself
through wires of anguish to the
fragile vibrations of my Womanness.

You called me beautiful,
licking my intimate scars as if they were merely
tiny fingers
scraped upon the sidewalks of a normal child-
hood—
accepting them . . .
allowing me to accept them—and you
within me
Slowly.

"See how much I love you?"
As my insides grow warm with bleeding,
you reply softly, soberly: "Yes . . . I know."
I can tell by your tears that you suddenly realize
you don't love me—or always knew.
Still, I need to not hate you—not now; so
before I can think anymore,

Dawn Bailiff
has "performed" her edgy confes-
sional verse in numerous solo shows,
poetry series and workshops, both
for live and television audiences.
Response to her edgy confessional
verse has been consistently positive
at many DelMarVa venues, includ-
ing: The Painted Bride Arts
Center and Robin's Bookstore,
Philadelphia; Enoch Pratt Free
Library and Eubie Blake Cultural
Center, Baltimore; and The Folger
Shakespeare Library Reading
Series, Washington D.C. Most
recently, Dawn's work has appeared
in *Inside MS*, *The Mad Poet's
Review*, volume 5 of *In Good
Company*, and volumes 19, 20 and
21 of *The Poet's Domain*. The
musical quality of her poetry stems
from her years as an internationally
acclaimed classical pianist. She is
a graduate of the Peabody Conservatory.

Dawn Bailiff

I pull your face closer to my lips, waiting for
your tears
to purify
my aching soul . . .

but all they do is wash me back to my old self,
before the blood but not
before the bruises.


## To My Father

I succeeded in escaping the reality of you—
it wasn't difficult—
but, somehow, I could never elude
the illusion of you.

I tried—melting my memory into a forward-
moving stream,
oozing to seek a more practicable mold—
recycled
like liquid metal,
making myself reusable.

Just like the husband who followed you
to the bottom of my darkest ocean,
only to drown in the pools of desire, with an
edge.

Many since have resurfaced, unscarred,
upon more temperate shores,
making me obsolete.

Just as *you* still try to do, but never can,
for I am as eternal in you
as you are in me,
gnawing slowly—
a tapeworm of the soul.

I tried to kill *my* worm.
I tried to burn you from me with
rivers that sizzled

Dawn Bailiff

but I only almost lost myself. Almost.
And then I had to come back.

Come back to you through Freudian fathers in
gray-flannel,
their pretensions of liberation suffocating
as a cloud of barbiturates,

for I reject their brand of freedom—
freedom to conform to feelings I should never
have to feel,
freedom to serve perceptions, not realities,
freedom to run into their arms and call them
*Daddy*.

## The Winter of Disease

I watch the sun descending
and I think:
so many endings,
beginnings—
moments smacked upon the bottom only once
to breathe
and then
inhaling amniotic fluids and so drowning
dying
trying to regain a former consciousness—
or lack of consciousness—
preferring certainty in crawling
to the *chance* of someday
walking.

Endings, I remember when you said "Good-bye,"
and I, not yet knowing how solitary
I could be—how strong—
cried: "Please love me! I'm really
good—I just get ugly sometimes,
sometimes, when I cannot love myself—
sometimes, when I feel I'm dying . . . "
It didn't matter.

Dawn Bailiff

It didn't matter that the roses
you had given me had
died, leaving only
withered longings:
the novelty of Baby's Breath turned stale—
the pride of crystal shattered into plastic cola
bottles.
Illusions shedding layers
like deceased petals crying
upon wooden desktops:
Desires solidified by EGO.

The sky grows dark,
and I am sickened
by the very transience of things—
of light, of love,
of my own life rapidly sifting back
into the Womb of Eternity—
of my petals withering in blackness,
never with sufficient time to thrive purple
in completion—
only drooping from the frost of pain,
their tired heads of stasis
bowing in acceptance or defeat,
all tenderness of color frozen
by the winter of disease.

Dawn Bailiff

# Kristallnacht

Violated by an unknown hammer,
my car windows lay in pieces—
translucent, severed, crystallized
by unforgiving hardness.

These inviolate violations
are too common now
that I have a "special" license plate.
Some people just don't like the handicapped.

This glass is hard to dream against
as it splinters in my soul like disbelief.

This cell in which I try to write
is just as sharp—icy in its strippedness.

My tiny slab of bed looks out over a set of
wooden bunks
that remind me of the sleeping quarters
at Dachau.

I was just a young girl
when I visited the concentration camp
where so many of my people had died—
aunts who were about my age,
whose eyes and minds, vaginas, souls
were sliced and slivered by the Aryan edge.
Some people just don't like the Jews.

I snapped a picture of those boxed beds
because it was a strange comfort.

The interlacing formula of sticks
rattled in my brain like bones
that would not burn,
until the hollow sound of my own wood
against the unforgiving hardness
blocked them out.

My own box of pain was wrapped and waiting;
before this, I never knew
that ripping paper screamed
like breaking glass.

*Doris C. Baker*

Principal of an American army
school in Germany after World
War II; master's degree from the
University of Michigan; author of
a novel, *The Originals*, 2002;
poetry, short fiction, articles, and
essays in *The Poetry Society of
Virginia Anthology* 2003, *The
Virginia Gazette, Virginia
Adversaria, Pegasus Review,
Skylark, Sensations Magazine,
German Life Magazine* and other
publications; member of two
Virginia Beach writers groups.

## Chronicles

Canyon walls narrow
   around uncertain feet
   cracklebones.
Turn back to lost years
   moon ripples in the grass.
   Are you listening?

Horizon arrow red-orange
   points to darkness,
   remembrance burning.
Midnight sun dips and rises,
   shimmers above the Arctic
   flood of layered pearls.

Greek caiques tilt decks
   into meltemi storms of the Aegean,
   prophecies from the temple of Apollo.
Ocean surf sifting sand
   at water's edge,
   curlews on tiptoe retreat.

Flight of yellow birds shiver
   aspen leaves staccato
   sky music singing.
Strawberry sugar juice
   spills honey-sweet
   aroma of summer fruit.

Doris C. Baker

Trailing vines tangle feet
    of fallen god statues,
      barter for daggers in Angkor Wat.
Restless stars above the embers
    of desert campfires lure
      camels mumbling to the moon.

Are you listening
    sun shadows on the wall?
    I don't tell all.
There were so many kinds of love
    among the lonely islands and in
    the traffic of Singapore and Rome.

## Climbing Back In

For a moment
a mere blink of the eye
I knew how to fly.

And iridescent feathers,
never imagined,
dressed unsuspected wings.

For a heartbeat in time
I let gravity slide—
rode thermal drafts
to breathless heights
and left the weighted
world behind.

But I could not
hold on to the dream
or it could not
hold on to me.

Now here I am, climbing
back in
to my old familiar
fitted skin—
    wings clipped
earthbound again.

*lorraine m Benedetto*

Child of the 60s born and raised in the Northeast, moved to Tidewater Virginia in '92, transferred to Wilmington, North Carolina in the fall of 2001, where I have begun to notice the influence of water and tides becoming more and more entrenched in my writing. Writer of poetry and short stories—with an ongoing attempt to complete my first full-length novel. Previously published in *The Poet's Domain*, volumes 17, 19, and 20; *Beacon*; and *Poetic Voices*.

lorraine m Benedetto

## Night Music

Alone in her room
she dreams of machines
encased in cocoons
growing gossamer wings.

Three floors below
Bourbon Street blues slide from the stage
as the saxophone plays a mournful refrain,
each note an homage to unfiltered pain.

Four doors down, lost in the howl
of a Gibsonesque riff,
leather laced gin seduces the room
with her unbridled youth.

And the night moves on
in search of fresh meat.

Alone in her bed she
tosses and turns;
fighting the greed
of the moon's iron rule.

## Kitchen Philosophy

Mother said
"We are the shadows
our ancestors cast."

I can still hear
my father's laugh
as he rose from his chair
and leaned over
to kiss her nose.

"No," he said,
"we are the tapestry
they wove."

Her smile was his
reward.

lorraine m Benedetto

## Window Seat

I love these days dressed in Ansel Adams gray
(as if color and sound, exhausted by the ardor
of spring's complex demands
had chosen to sleep in—
leaving billows and tendrils of ground fog
free to decorate the day).

A pot of tea, instead of a cup,
hair unbrushed,
night's sleep still lingering
in muscles not yet stretched,
I wrap myself in an old fleece robe;
settle into my rocking chair
and watch the tide slowly ebb
beneath the feet of salt marsh trees.

Maybe it's the quiet, the muffled isolation
that takes me to my secrets,
or maybe it's the ghostly light
reminding me I'm haunted
by a yesterday that's dressed this way.
Or maybe I just can't resist
the wisps of tempting memories
that always seem to permeate
such pallid scenery.

Time has a way of getting lost
when melancholy comes to tea.

But there's dishes in the kitchen sink
and the checkbook needs a balancing;
the laundry's gotten mountainous
and the teapot's down to unread leaves.

Just in time the sun checks in
to see what mischief the fog's got to
and watch me shake the morning off—
stretching out those unstretched limbs
as I make my way to the bathroom door.

lorraine m Benedetto

## How Can I Explain It To You When
## I Don't Understand It Myself

It wasn't a lie, exactly—
more of a temporary truth.
Not like the kind that are absolute.

Think of it as a localized suspension
of the laws of gravity
that left me free to believe in wings,

or the reckless and unplanned release
of a genie wisely bottled up.

Name it the insanity
of undistinguished waking dreams
that camouflaged reality,

or a prisoner's vain rattling
of the chains of history

    or the fervent prayer
    of an atheist
    who's thrice denied
    the face of God.

## Refuge
After returning from Southside Virginia

Stopping in that quiet place,
Peeling back the wrinkled skin,
To check inevitable damage
By looking deep within,

I can say I danced with rabbits,
Chased blue lizards up the wall,
At night lolled on the porch swing
Listening to the apples fall.

My Friend, so well-accomplished,
Would you share this glass of wine?
Can you claim the ledger of your days
More worthy than is mine?

## The Queen Bed

Last night I slept all over
My bed, the queen bed
My long-lost lover
Declared I should buy.

Where is he now? It's
A question I sometimes
Ask myself as I drift
To middle-aged dreams.

I have taken a striped cat
Into my bed or, rather,
Onto my bed on a
Night-to-night trial basis.

He likes to wander
And curls up in various
Spots on the Royal
Barge of Slumber.

*Patricia L. Beneš*

is a writer and consultant for higher education. Born in Baltimore, she has spent most of her life in Pennsylvania, and now resides in Phoenixville, Pa. Pat earned a bachelor's degree from Oberlin College and a master's degree from West Chester University of Pennsylvania. She studied and worked in France and Austria. In her professional career, she has served a large public university system and three private colleges, most recently as Vice President for Institutional Advancement, Saint Paul's College in Lawrenceville, Virginia. Pat has three grown sons, Ben, Andy and Petr, all musicians.

Patrícia L. Beneš

Some nights he just
Yawns, looks up from
His nap on the sofa as I
Climb upstairs to bed.

So I slide between
Flannel sheets alone,
Wiggle my toes for warmth,
Then grab a pillow.

Clutching it to my
Belly comforts me like
The memory of carrying
A new life inside.

After counting my
Heirlooms, the crown jewels,
Knotty fingers gently
Relax, extend.

I pray to see
Indigo behind my
Eyelids that last second
Before I fall.

## Portable Drugstore

I am a walking pharmacy,
the drugs I take number thirty-three.
At times I admit it gets confusing,
but those pesky pills find it amusing.

The ills for which the pills are for,
are inconvenient, nothing more.
So, here's my pharmaceutical menu,
clearly an addict's doping venue.

Lipitor for clogged arteries,
    Imodium for runs and wateries.
Fosamax for bones grown weak,
    Motrin for knees that creak.
Cardizem for a heart with extra beats,
    Prozac for a mood that's bleak.
Afrin when my nose gets clogged and stuffy,
    Cognex when my memory's fuzzy.

Asacol for my intestinal tract,
    Mucinex when I cough and hack.
Sulfa for pimples on my nose,
    Desenex for fungus on my toes.
Diamox for vascular hypertension,
    Sup-hose for varicose prevention.
Oxybutyrin for a bladder that's weak,
    Atenalol for a heart valve leak.

I could go on, and on, and on,
but my throat is dry, my voice is gone.
My feet are sore, I'm weak and tired,
Very tense and highly wired.

Besides, I have to pee,
so p a–l e e z, excuse me.

Barry R. Berkey, M.D.

a freelance writer and psychiatrist, graduated Phi Beta Kappa from Washington and Jefferson College and received his M.D. from the University of Pittsburgh School of Medicine. He has had eight books published (some coauthored with his wife), four for adults and four for children. Dozens of his essays and articles have appeared in the *Washington Post*, *The Philadelphia Inquirer*, *Potomac Review*, *Continuum Review*, *Stitches*, *Human Sexuality*, the *American Journal of Psychiatry*, among others. His work has been published by Live Wire Press in *The Poet's Domain*, volumes 16, 18, 21, and 22.

Barry R. Berkey, M.D.

## Upside-down Cake

Why couldn't I have been a chocolate layer cake?
or even better, a birthday or wedding cake?
Gladly I'd have switched with a pineapple cake,
alas, my fate is sealed, for I am what I am
what I am.

I make the best of an impossible quest,
as a freakish outcast who fails every test.
Popular for all the wrong reasons unfurled,
an infamous weirdo from a baker's dream world.

Bearer of genetic mutations gone asunder,
a thalidomide wonder of baking dough blunder.
To me the world twists in total reverse,
a state for which I can't plan or rehearse.

So take a quick peek at the inversion I see,
then for sure you will know the preposterous me.
In my world:
    the weather forecast predicts an uppour;
    an old man falls up a flight of stairs;
    astronomers watch rising stars;
    pianists play downright pianos;
    podiatrists fix outgrown toenails;
    when I get sick to my stomach, I throw down;
    the apple doesn't rise far from the tree;
    a cop angrily calls a perp an upright liar;
    clerks at shoe stores help you try off shoes;
    equestrians go horsebelly riding;
    carpenters hammer out nails;
    firemen put in fires;
    and so it goes or, rather, so it comes.

My turvy-topsy universe is wholly regrettable,
detailing why I'm an unforgettable edible.

## In a Mountain Stream

I put my feet in a mountain stream.
The water gurgled and ran through my toes
And asked, "Who is this stranger?"
Nobody knows.

Nobody knows where I've been, what's my name.
Who I was yesterday isn't the same.
Nobody knows what I've done 'til this minute.
I came to a stream and I put my feet in it.

## I Am Away from My Desk

*Laura J. Bobrow*

(b.1928, Mount Vernon, N.Y.)
has been described as having "the
mind of a poet and philosopher,
the wit of a comedian, and the
voice and diction of an orator,"
useful adjuncts in her career as a
storyteller. Laura uses poetry to
enhance her telling, often putting
well-known stories or parts of sto-
ries into verse. In addition to her
"serious" work, Laura's award-
winning children's poems, light
verse, and lyrics have been pub-
lished in many venues. In 1961,
referring to her poetry for children,
Louis Untermeyer called her the
"American Milne." She is a resi-
dent of Leesburg, Va.

Not for you, old woman,
This early snowfall that was once your joy.
Unwittingly you have acquired
Dignity with age.

Not for you, old woman, they say.
But why should I not build
a massive snow cat with carrot nose?

Not for you, old woman?
What the heck.
Maybe I will do that right now.

## View from the Bathroom Sink

Faces come in varied sizes
And funny shapes, like crackerjack prizes.
Hair is there, or else it's missing.
Lips designed for lemon kissing. . . .

Everyone, except for me,
Has some peculiarity.
Mirror, mirror, it's not I.
You're looking at some other guy.

Laura J. Bobrow

## The Game's Not Over

I placed the cards to play at solitaire.
Straight edge to edge they pressed me close around
And stared at me, the soldiers and the kings,
Red queens and knaves, the saints and feudal lords.
"Too bad, my friend," a joker called out loud.
"Play out your luck, but then you forfeit all.
For win or lose or draw, you'll wind up dead."

Not yet, I say. I am my daddy's child,
And he lived long, and healthy for his years.
The game is done when every card is played.
He kept the ace of spades beneath his sleeve.

## Big-City Girl

(acrostic)

Nightly in Gotham Town,
East of the continent,
West of the ocean lanes,
Yell of a jackhammer, rumble of subway trains.
Over the functional, fractional dissonance
Runs Atalanta,
Keen for the race.

Now throw the apples down,
Each one more eloquent.
Who would not stop for this,
Yield to the lures of a jeweled metropolis?
Only Manhattan has music and magic and
Room for a huntress
Kept from the chase.

## Major Decision

Wombs are warm. The air is chilly.
Those who trade, therefore, are silly.
Yet I know without a doubt
I'm awfully glad that I came out.

## An Ode to Found Money

I think that had I saved each bit
of money I have found,
from young childhood until now
in my sixth decade,
I would have enough to take a trip, say,
or buy a few armfuls of books
or a fine 'scope to spot an elusive bird
but I have simply spent them freely
on the next temptation to present itself,
ice cream, perhaps
or a smooth yellow pencil
or a chocolate cream or two
in a white paper bag
from the corner store.

## Essence

What will still matter in fifteen years more
that figures large in my life of today?
Poems by others that help me explore
the why and the wherefore that I cannot say.
Poems of mine which I trust will still spring
from tidbits of passion that tug at my sleeve.
Persons connected by family's wing
or by friendships in rings linked by laughter
and grief.
Wind on my face as I walk in the morning,
birdsong that spills into calls of good cheer,
taste of ripe mango with juice overflowing,
strawberries tart with fine wine in glass clear.
My health to allow me to indulge and endure,
in fifteen brief years these will still be secure.

*jan bohall*

studies and writes in a poetry
workshop during half of each year,
and wrestles words into poems on
themes that she hopes are univer-
sal. With upstate New York roots,
she was educated in nursing and
has retired from a public health
position. Her work has been pub-
lished in *The Poet's Domain*, vol-
umes 20 and 21; *Passager: A
Journal of Remembrance and
Discovery*; and *The Orange
County Register* of Santa Ana,
California.

## We Were Poets

One day, you'll say back then
we were poets, stealing morning
light to sprinkle in rhymed or

unrhymed verse so proud that
even little words sparkled
to dazzle us and us alone.

Back then, you'll say we penned
our journey across pages too
brief to hold a full heart's truth,

too fragile to keep the pain from
seeping through the soul's
sentimental words of faith.

You'll say we learned that comfort
is the mind's deceit, robbing it of
yearning for thoughts yet unwritten

and untested, like the just born
child that hears but does not
speak its own language.

Back then, you'll say we knew the
eagle perching in the pine tree who
captured human words of praise,

in measured verse before
he rose in graceful, silent flight
to dazzle us and us alone.

Barbara Brady

a native of Washington, D.C., is a
writer and artist living at *Scotia* in
Virginia on the Western shore of
the Chesapeake. Over the years,
her poetic offerings have appeared
in many literary publications. The
adjacent poem is dedicated to her
kindred poets whose verse inspires
this volume of *The Poet's
Domain*.

## Bob-White?

"and the quails
Whistle about us their spontaneous cries."
—*Wallace Stevens*

There was a quaint whistling about me in the
wheat,
Its intention seemingly connected to my feelings.
Alone, I halted the air and breathed it in as if
To mollify a memory. I spoke aloud,
Telling how the neighbors gathered together
On a rug-covered porch; wooden chairs
In circular display; voices telling stories.
One seat vacant on the swing. Could it be mine?
But I was only four, an age when visions flutter,
Angel-like, there to fan away the pain
of being quaint. Or so it was that I believed
When hiding in a room where the air was warm,
Electric fans verboten to the child. But maybe
I could tell about the time my brother, Bob,
Snatched a bag of peanuts from my hand, and ran,
Laughing, as if he challenged me to follow.
He didn't see the hole, and the peanuts dropping
As he ran, while this little sister picked them up
And loaded all the fallen peanuts in her dress.
What a funny story that would be to tell.
But in excitement I forgot my handicap. To them
My lisping tongue would be the source of
humor,
My neighbors' taunting and demeaning twit:
"you thilly ugly duckling! Thilly, thilly duckling."
Here the shame of imperfection overpowers
until
Spontaneous cries erupt. Something was
Reclaiming me, something phantom-like,
angelic:
It was the quail's connection, dulcet and articulate:
"Always accent with a smile on the upward
pitch: Bob-White?"

*Beatrice Bright*

(b.1925, Elgin, Ill.) is a retired
musician who lives in the Akron
Borough of Lancaster County, Pa.
As an ageless enthusiast of the
Arts, she hopes to never let up on
opening her home for poetry and
musical soirees. Her poems appear
in many regional and national pub-
lications. She is also the author of
a limited-edition of a chapbook,
*Shades of the Battlefield*, written
during her weekly morning walks
through Bull Run Battlefield when
she was a resident of Manassas,
Va. This is her sixth appearance in
*The Poet's Domain*.

## Twilight Calling

Blue reaches out like a lullaby
humming you home, muffling the drone of
engines idling, wheels grinding, calling
quick leave the car, leave the phone
to hold the last light
before the night calls you to the table

Come, sit with me and you will see
dark limbs passing secrets,
like sisters at bedtime, laughing,
they wrap you in their arms,
telling you stories of beeches and oaks
long into the winter

Come, slip into velvet bark
ride the driftwood of your heart
across the waves of celestine
into the swell of indigo and
feel me quicken, into
the still of twilight

*Laura Brighton*

mother and social worker, is
revising her life to make room
for unfinished poems. Writing
poetry is a vehicle for personal and
spiritual growth as well as an impor-
tant tool in her work as a psychother-
apist. She believes that poetry
connects us to that still voice within
that has the power to heal and
integrate our many hidden selves.
In her poetry, Laura explores light,
color, and the polarities of daily
life. She has recently been pub-
lished in several anthologies.

Laura Brighton

## The Light in Your Kitchen

I am the light in your kitchen
you know the one
that follows you in the morning
lifting you from musty sleep
to find magnolias
shining in your dish rack
I lead you into shimmering dust
to counters lighting up
the patterns you rely on
from sink to coffee pot
I bring you the equinox
in my trajectory
a slant on your day
A story of light in the ordinary.

# The Fiddler in the Graveyard

In a still and quiet graveyard,
Where the stones stood row on row,
There in the awesome stillness,
Where no breath of breeze would blow,
Where the lost and long-forgotten
Were lying cold and low,
Some high-pitched notes rang out like gunshots,
As somebody drew a bow.

And, looking across the hillside,
I saw a strange young man.
He was sitting on a headstone,
And then I saw him stand.
And, rosining up his bow a bit,
He then began to play,
Such high-pitched notes and brilliant
That the clouds all blew away.

He played with driving rhythm,
Tunes that had a lilting lift.
He played so well and wildly,
He had the rarest gift.
Thus he played about an hour,
For those who could not hear,
Until I finally approached him,
And I inquired, "Sir,

"Why do you ply your talent
In this unseemly place?
When those you play for cannot hear you,
Your talent goes to waste."
He replied, "This is the fiddle
My father gave to me,
And alas! That dear and kindly man
Now lies beneath our feet.

*Lilli Lee Buck*

(b. Feb. 25, 1950, in Butler, Pa.)
the daughter of Lt. Col. Shelburne
T. and Edith Buck, now resides
near Bristol, Va. She was graduated
from the College of William and
Mary with a B.A. in anthropology
in 1972, and an M.Ed. degree in
1984. An astrologer, musician,
singer, and poet, she has published
poetry in many anthologies. An
animal rights advocate, she has a
small private animal shelter. She
works for human rights and world
peace. Her goals are to save lives
and souls. In her poetry, she seeks
to uplift and edify as well as to
entertain.

Lilli Lee Buck

"As we huddled by the fire
    Many a cold and winter's night,
He played it by the hour,
    And it was our chief delight.
And when he'd hang the fiddle up,
    He'd take me on his knee,
And before he put me into bed,
    He used to promise me

"That he'd teach me all his music,
    And when I became a man,
I'd be a fine musician,
    Because I had his hands.
And when he grew old, with trembling hands,
    He called me to his side,
And gave me this, his fiddle,
    A month before he died.

"And I refused to take it,
    As it was his joy and pride,
But until I agreed to have it,
    He would not be satisfied.
And now that he's locked forever
    In death's cold and wintry night,
My love for him which cannot die
    Will be his firelight,

"And the music which he gave to me
    I'll echo back to him,
And if he can hear from Heaven,
    He'll know it's Little Jim."
As I walked back down the hillside,
    A tear was in my eye.
I heard the fiddle dance and sing,
    I heard the fiddle cry.

A jig, a reel, a planxty,
    And then a sad slow air.
As two stars fell in the sunset,
    I left him playing there.

Lilli Lee Buck

## Dancing Fairies

Down along the fence line, along the row of trees,
    Where the dogwood blossoms
    Are tossing in the breeze,
Down among the violets and buttercups are seen,
    Fairies, fairies, dancing on the green.

Dancing in a circle, dancing in a line,
    Dancing in a figure eight, dancing all in time,
    While the birds are singing,
And humming are the bees,
    Fairies, fairies, dancing through the trees.

See their wings of gossamer,
    Like hummingbirds in flight.
    See their footsteps leaping,
    Gracefully and light.
See their hair of sunshine, with a sylvan sheen,
    Fairies, fairies, dancing on the green.

In the dew of morning, by the light of dawn,
    Fairies, fairies, dancing on the lawn.
    Down among the dandelions,
Drinking in the dew,
    Fairies, fairies, dancing for you.

Lilli Lee Buck

## Sashes and Bows

I first met my true love at the county fair ball,
    Out of three hundred ladies, the fairest of all,
Her eyes like pure water, her cheeks like the rose,
    And her long hair was tied up
With sashes and bows.

The pie she had baked there
    Had won the first prize.
And the blue of her ribbon
    Was the hue of her eyes.
I sampled her cobbler in the bakery rows,
    And her apron was tied up
With sashes and bows.

I danced with my darling
    Both easy and slow.
She was lithe as a willow and soft as a doe.
    With her head on my shoulder,
In the lantern's soft glow,
    Her long hair was tied up
With sashes and bows.

We whirled round and round there
    To the fiddles' sweet whine.
It was then I decided
    That she must be mine.
I won the best prize there, as everyone knows,
    And she tied up my heartstrings
With sashes and bows.

## Spirits on the Wind

Stealthily they glide,
Seeking port on foreign soil.
A snake slips into the creek.
Around them, birds are still.

There a spot, perhaps a bank.
Their uninvited kayaks push through brush,
Fighting for a chance to land.
There'd been a path worn up the hill,
Past now-skeleton Barn and Cook Lodge,
Between Stables and Quarters, to the Big House.
Today, tall, sharp grass; ivy; a bird-spawned tree,
Where slave feet once marked ways toward fields
And the Ice House at the turning pond.

The Big House stood determined, propped by
ancient trees,
Doors proper locked though windows beckoned,
Glass and panes long gone, luring the pair
toward darkness.
He took her hand and led her through,
Back to high ceiling rooms with hand-carved
molding,
A Morning Room now ruled by vines.
One chimney fallen, the gap displaying foot-
thick walls.
They kissed amidst the wreckage,
Warmed each with thoughts of other.

Hornets break the silence.
Listening now, more sounds, perhaps a wail,
Voices singing past their pain of homes they'd
never see.
Laughter, giggles, elocution lessons,
A newborn's call, chords from a parlor piano.
When spirits range, the wind takes note.
Air shifts. Shadows fall.
Memories and footsteps are passing into time.
Tea will not be served this day.

Janine Burns

was born in Washington, D.C.,
and earned degrees from St.
Mary's College, Notre Dame,
Indiana, and Johns Hopkins
University in Baltimore, Md.
Historically, Janine's writing has
focused on speeches, articles, and
business publications. Moving at a
more relaxed pace today, she enjoys
writing for new markets. Her mono-
logue "Richard" was incorporated
into *Life on the Chesapeake*, pro-
duced at the Kimball Theater in
Williamsburg, Va., and "Assam," a
short story, was published in vol-
ume five of *In Good Company*.

## My Soul and Me

The soul is the essence of my being
I shall die when it leaves me.
Deep lies the mystery of life,
Death and immortality.

Perhaps in a dream, I saw myself,
Lying motionless on the ground,
A lifeless body, an empty shell.
People were weeping all around.

I wanted to tell them I was there,
I tried to speak—no sound came.
I felt the joy of being free—
They kept on calling out my name.

I must have drifted up above
For suddenly I could see
A brilliant light! And in the midst
A dazzling figure—who was he?

When I opened my eyes I wept,
Tried to go back to my dream, in vain,
I yearned to relive that vision of light
But my soul was imprisoned once again.

## Today

Today I like to think of pretty things
Of golden sunsets and of angels' wings,
Dream of dancing in a wispy dress
Floating in a cloud of happiness.

I love to feel the soft breeze in my hair,
And wander, carefree in the pungent air.
Today I see my spirit flying high
Today I want to laugh and not to cry.

*Sheila Cardano*

a native of England, now resides
on the Eastern Shore of Virginia.
Poet, playwright, artistic director of
Arts Enter Cape Charles, she
writes and directs her original
plays at the Palace Theatre for this
non-profit organization. Her
poems have appeared in most of
the volumes of *The Poets Domain*.

Sheila Cardano

## Echoes

Weirdly, from an unknown space,
    I heard my childish laughter
Echoing strangely with the cries
    Of sobbing, which came after.

    Poignantly recalling how my
    Skies were always blue.
    Gloom and doom did not exist.
    Every dream came true.

Odd to listen to the sounds
That time had washed away,
But with my eyes I could not see—
That child of yesterday.

## Her Mountain

She never intended to climb a mountain.
It came to her.
Unexpected and unwelcome,
suddenly in front of her without warning.

A normal day began.
An afternoon visit with her doctor.
Cancer.
An old office clock ticked one second
and an entire life changed.

She calmly turned to begin her journey.
The climb was steep and treacherous as
she fought desperately to survive each step.
She found few resting places along the way,
only narrow ledges with sharp rocks.
But on those ledges there was no pain.
The sun shone on her face
and she laughed out loud.

Then the mountain called again
and she knew she must continue.
She did not look back as she climbed,
for she knew she would never again return.

Her body weakened with the journey, and
often she dreamed of the other side.
Nearing the peak, she could almost
touch the clouds.
Release was replacing pain.

She stood tall atop her private mountain,
knowing her journey was through.
With a sigh, she gracefully leapt
and then took flight.
And her joy filled the heavens.

*Alison Chapman*

is a native of Smithfield, Va.,
where she lives with her husband
and two children, of whom she is
more proud than she could ever
put into words. She is an elemen-
tary school teacher and loves shar-
ing her passion for music with her
students. Her poetry is inspired by
life, with all its unpredictability.
She is honored that two of her first
published poems are among those
she wrote for her mother, who
encouraged her in all she endeav-
ored, and she dedicates them with
much love to her brothers.

Alison Chapman

## Leaving Home

This old body has served me well
And I'll bid it a fond farewell.
Two feet that ran and played
And pedaled a bicycle that was way too big.
The same feet walked down the aisle
On my wedding day.
Two hands that learned work and play
And never could master the art of sewing.
The same hands held my precious newborn
babies.
Eyes that saw the smiles of friends and family,
And shed tears when the same were lost.
Most of all, a heart that has been steady,
Beating fast with excitement and joy,
Sometimes aching with pain
But always,
Always,
Loving.

## Unexpected Journey

Well, here I am.
I'm not sure how I got here.
The map I carefully planned for my life
did not include this destination.
I began that journey so long ago.
Along the way, there were detours.
Many of the roads I meant to take
were closed. I thought I was supposed
to travel those highways,
but it wasn't meant to be.
Occasionally, a scenic route would
lure me away from the main road,
causing me to lose time
and perhaps some opportunities.
Yet the scenery was indeed breathtaking.
Reality,

Alison Chapman

or necessity,
or sometimes failure,
would pull me back to the main highway.

There were times when travelers around me
forced me to slow down to a crawl,
or even come to a complete stop.
Other times they would speed by me
while I struggled to move at all,
searching desperately for directions.
The worst, though, were the crashes,
unexpected jolts that stopped me,
knocked me down, or threw me over
onto another path, sore and bruised,
forced to travel a different route.
God, I hated those.

But my traveling continued.
Life continued.
Now I am not even sure where I put
that old map. I have long since
discarded it, realizing its uselessness,
though still remembering
the dreams that created it.
No, the journey was not at all what I had
planned.
Yet I look around this place that is my life
with all its wrong turns and imperfections.
I am surrounded by beauty
and I am at peace.

## Pumping Iron

Two days a week after work,
    instead of driving home
I travel on to the gym,
    in hopes of reducing aging's flab,
sculpting my body with toned muscles.
As I change from my professional disguise
into my workout clothes,
    I hear splashings
from the indoor pool, populated at all times,
    it seems,
with half a dozen men over seventy.
Today they must be practicing their cannonballs.
Great explosions of flesh slapping water, echoing
exclamations of triumph, fill the beige-tiled space.

I try to time my workouts carefully—
    after the gruntings
of testosterone-laden body-builders, before
workouts of the depressingly fit twenties set.
When I arrive, there are usually just a few folks
of around my own age—some flabbier, some
who have been at this longer, looking the way I
hope to—someday—in how many months or
years?
The huge room is redolent of a day's worth
of straining bodies.
Fans spin frantically overhead.

I pull on my fingerless gloves, sling a towel
over my shoulder, take a long sip from my
insulated water bottle, and begin.
My eyes measure the seats of the exercise bikes—
by now I can tell on which one I can warm up
without laborious adjustments of saddle.
After ten minutes of spinning legs, I move
to the weight machines. As I push and pull
    and lift and row,

*Leslie Clark*

earned her M.A. in English through the creative writing program at Old Dominion University and taught in Virginia for more than twenty years. Currently she is English faculty at Cochise College, Douglas Campus and online. Her poetry and short fiction have been widely published for more than twenty years. She and her husband live in Cochise County, Arizona, and witness daily clashes of dreams vs. reality associated with the proximity of the Mexican border. Leslie is editor/publisher of a quarterly online poetry journal, *Voices of the Wind*, http://geclark.mystarband.net

Leslie Clark

I try to imagine my muscles inflating, hardening,
with each repetition of movement. I've increased
weight twice now, added sets, varied exercises.
I move smoothly through the routine—legs,
    arms, abs.
Work, work, hoping for the miracle to happen.

## Writing Teacher's Face

After thirty years of teaching,
there are parentheses
between my brows, engraved
by countless hours
of squinting over stacks of essays.
My eyes are framed by
black pen-stroke lines.
A row of exclamation marks appears
over my dash of a mouth
Tiny red squiggles are critical
comments across my cheeks.
Nightly, I sigh as I rub cream
into papery skin.
But each morning,
when I greet my students,
my face again becomes
a beautiful thesis statement.

## Sonnet for a Sinner

My sister-in-law said I was selfish
to spend the five thousand Daddy left me
that way. My preacher said I'd better wish
I didn't go straight to hell. God's mercy
could save my soul if I would give the church
its ten percent before it was too late.
Everybody knows I don't care that much
about treasures beyond the pearly gate.
I practically live in that swimming pool
out there. I can watch through the window
neighbors wishing they were lying in the cool
blue water. And when the dust from the coal
trucks covers it with a thick scum of black, I
just take my scoop and go on out back.

*Shirley F. Cox*

born in Grundy, Va., recently
retired after teaching English,
drama, and creative writing at
Randolph-Henry High School
and at Southside Virginia
Community College. Her poetry
has won prizes in the Poetry
Society of Virginia contests,
including a prize in '04, and in the
Ohio Poetry Society contest. Her
poetry has been published in
*Poetry Motel* and in the latest edi-
tion *of Poetry Society of Virginia
Anthology of Poems.* An avid
golfer, she lives in Farmville, Va.
This is her seventh appearance in
*The Poet's Domain.*

## Independence Day

The afternoon my mother pulled
scratchy wool leggings
onto my raw skin,
slipped elastic over my heels,
forced boots over my balled up socks,
bundled me into nine layers of
suffocating protection,
and told me to go outside
and play
I knew I would not live like this forever
knew someday I would run through the snow
naked
throw myself backward and make snow angels
that leapt up, fluttered, followed
where ever I led,
dance
in the sunshine
abandon shoulds and oughts
unzip my soul
to the wind and cold
toss
scratchy wool leggings
itchy plaid scarf
ice-clotted mittens
onto a snowbank
in the form of my body
shedding my skin
forever.

*Terry Cox-Joseph*

(b.1957, St. Paul, Minn.) is an artist, author, and editor, freelancing from her home in Newport News, Va. She is a former newspaper reporter and editor, and has had one book of nonfiction published, *Adjustments*, 1993, and is working on a novel called *Barren*. She was the coordinator for the annual Christopher Newport University Writers' Conference and contest for ten years.

Terry Cox-Joseph

## My Own Skin

Give me bittersweet dark chocolate to sink my
teeth into,
the soft strains of Paganini,
the wriggling ruff of a devoted collie,
a stack of novels with lines so well crafted
I'm swept away by a literary tsunami,
and I will never want to die,
or think I have already died
and departed
to a blissful afterlife

and then
give me your hand
and I'll remember
who I am.

## First Born

The first time I stared
into your unblinking sapphire eyes
heard your first whimper
stroked your matted black hair
touched your sticky vernix caseosa-covered
cheek
memorized your entire being
in the blink of a supernova,
sighed with exhaustion

I knew I'd come home.

## Just A Tree

The stormy trail I walked again
Seemed much the same as before
With ferns and mossy rocks to see
Along with every dripping tree
Until one fell in wind and rain
And came to rest in front of me
To change the scene ever more.

Not wishing to return soon home,
Around the crown seemed best to roam.
But, then, how could I truly say
Had I gone 'round the other way,
It would have been without the ease
Of stepping past a pile of leaves?

I walk in other places now
It just seems right to me somehow—
The old tree is at peace:
I'll let it lie—
A trail's a fitting place
For trees to die.

## Deer Talk

Where the woodland path I strode
Coursed across abandoned road—
Suddenly, a herd of deer!
They ran, then stopped—still quite near—
Ears outspread with eyes alert:
Who was I and would I hurt?
"It is our road," they seemed to say!
I understood, so went my way
Much wiser for the knowledge gained:
A good road is one not maintained.

*Frederick S. Crafts*

was born near Chicago in 1936. After living in California for a while, he moved with his family when he was eight years old to the Maryland suburbs of Washington, D.C. From this time through high school, Fred developed his strong appreciation for the natural world.

He attended the University of Michigan and worked for Texaco and the U.S. Dept. of the Interior. As a retired geologist, he now lives in a rural area of Northern Pa. He has been writing nature poetry for nearly twenty years.

## August Morning

Overnight the fisher
Wove a net
Taut from treeleaf
To grassblade,
Round, wide and glistening.
The angling rays of daybreak
Dance upon the quivering
Of winged things
Ensnared.

And as I walk through
Unaware,
A mantle thin and shimmering
With winged jewels
Is draped upon my hair.

Elaine Cramer

(born in Baltimore, Maryland) graduated from Drew University with a degree in anthropology. She lives in Hartly, Delaware. This is her fourth appearance in *The Poet's Domain*.

## Shared Affection

Between this blue sky and I
there flows such joy
beaming warm like the sunshine
the finches dart through,
quick as minnows
creasing clear water,
that I cannot call joy,
given so freely, cheap.

Although
joy wrenched from
the damp, cold fists of fog
might seem more dear.

Elaine Cramer

## A Drop of Youth

You spot her at once,
outgrowing her age with grace,
towering lithe and long limbed
above classmates in the play yard.
She tosses you her grin
over bobbing heads.
It arcs like the rainbow
you lunge to catch,
as if to cup a splash of gold
in work-worn hands—
a drop of youth.

She bothers
to tell you she's leaving.
"I want more than this,"
she says through her freckles.
It is not an apology at all—
no, not at all.
Called by challenge she scampers on,
shrugging off outgrown walls
with last fall's sweater.

## For Their Anniversary

I drove. My father sat
in the "leg room" seat.
Mother, in back, conversed
with the tone of our voices.
She could not pick out words
from the froth of tire noise and air.
Like a seer she spoke
the witness of our eyes—
spring-sign quickening the treeline.
Roads still familiar beneath the weight of
progress
lifted landmarks in welcome.
Eyes focused, heads nodded,
hearts raced with recognition.
Finally came family: the squall
of greetings, hugs and unspoken comparisons.
Finally came photographs and feasting,

Elaine Cramer

toasts and retold stories,
long farewells and promises.
Satisfied, Dad drowses.
Mom peers into the passing woods
hoping to snag the silhouette of a deer
as she weaves this reunion into their story.

## The Ice Cream Man

Beneath the afternoon sun shadows dozed.
Broiling streets blistered.
Honeysuckle nectar sizzled in its blossoms.
Bees stopped buzzing. Songbirds slept.
Dogs and cats rested their rivalries.
Even worms deep in the baked earth lan-
guished.
At the solemnity of high heat,
children lazed in shade
waiting and whispering.

He came every day. He came driving a truck
rubbed radiant as white patent leather.
On each side, a picture of an ice cream bar,
one bite taken.
Smoke billowed from the trailer when it
opened.
Smoke the color of an ice cube's core
curled down the side of the truck.
The man had a bell that jingled as it rang,
zing-zing, zing-Zing, Zing-Zing,
and the bell said
"Come to the corner, if you have a quarter."
It said all that in one sound,
ZING-ZING.

He waited, looking down at his wrist.
The children reveled in the nearness of sweet chill.
They felt their teeth making that bite,
the chocolate coating breaking,
cold vanilla spattering their tongues.
Dogs dreamed of licking
white meltings from the sidewalk.
He brought "good humor" every day.
The stagnant shade freshened at his arrival.

*Barbara McCreary Crann*

(b.1921, Evanston, Ill.) has written poetry since childhood. She attended Northwestern University's School of Speech and the Universities of Hawaii and Virginia. Currently, she is completing an autobiography detailing her early battle with mental illness and pioneering use of shock therapy in the late 30s. She resides in Alexandria, Va., with her husband. She served as president of the Alexandria branch of the National League of American Pen Women from 1995–1998.

# Valentine

"I live in my own private world," most recently you
    said,
as I changed a channel from my chair, and saw the
    top of your head.
"I know that," I responded, and watched your
    arm-chair spin,
"And sometimes," I quickly added . . . "sometimes
    you let me in."
For that's when you share and tease and support
And talk about golfing. (A wonderful sport!)
If I ask how your team played, your chair spins
    about . . .
and then in my heart I am feeling shut out.
BUT! When I talk about church and clowning
    and such,
I realize I've made a sensitive touch.
For years I have known that it turns you quite off
Just as it does when we talk about golf!
*I* cannot play it, *you* do not act
Or sing in my pageants . . . and that is a fact.
Yet somehow we've managed to balance our lives.
I've had but one husband, you've no other wives!
Love through our children, their children, our pride
And acceptance, concern . . . it never has died!
We're honest, and faithful, and not hard to please,
And we both love our dog, even though he has fleas
And flaws in his habits, he's always revealing
His sensitive, loving, rebellious dog-feeling.
Responding to voices, reacting to touch
And inclusion, confusion, and loves us so much!
So! With me eighty-three going on eight-four,
And you eighty-eight—yes! There is more!
We are closer than ever with faith in each other,
And the children who love us as father and mother,
And who, in their lives reach out to their own,
Reflecting the love that through years *we* have shown.
"I live in my own private world," said L.B.,
But for fifty-nine years, I know part of it's me!

## Return

The year's circle returns me
to the month of my birth.
I remember . . . but *can't* remember
an impossibility. Just born,
I'd know only the womb.

Perhaps the story often told me:
of banishment from my mother's room
to the hospital nursery
—my wailing annoyed her doctor—
made such a first memory, to harbor over
years!

Perhaps my *return* is my actual
Memory—reborn from the nursery
to my mother's arms, cradled then
the way the new moon holds
its whole self in the crescent of its curve.

I balance in the unstill airs
of long ago and now.

## The Snapshot

Captured
in another tourist's camera,
I start to apologize:
"Sorry,
you don't want me there . . ."
But already
I'm included in ephemera—
my *self* divided moves off
who knows where.

B. R. Culbertson

(b.1929, Lynchburg, Va.) is a
conjugal facilitator living in
Blacksburg, Virginia. Her work
has appeared in several volumes of
*The Poet's Domain*, as well as *The
Lyric, Southern Poetry Review,
The Comstock Review, Passager,
The Sow's Ear, Potpourri, Blue
Unicorn*, and elsewhere.

B. R. Culbertson

# The Telling Time

Fall leaves attend the rustlings of the night.
*(At summer's end, the mice played without sound,*
*the moon filled out behind a veil of trees*
*green, even in the dark . . .)*

Now not a step is taken without crisp
announcement of a coming; every brittle
breaking tells of deer or possum, mouse,
or even beetle heading for a home.

Leaves loose their hold inevitably.
For me, time clicks by fast as a quick shift
of air ticks drifts of walnut leaves onto the tin
roof.
Tomorrow more skeletons of trees,

more bared bones. Even so,
I'd like some guarantee
I'll see the same sad season
    one more year.

# Driving

My Daddy thought if I would drive
I needed more to just survive.

I'd have to learn to fix the car—
The names of parts, and where they are.

I've driven cars for forty years,
O'er miles of roads, in all the gears.

I've driven up and down the coast.
I've driven lots more miles than most,

But fix a car, no, no, not me. . . .
That's where I'll never, never be!

*Alice C. Daniels*

was born (1926) in Cleveland,
Ohio, educated in Virginia,
including Mary Washington
College, Fredericksburg. Now
retired, she worked for the U.S.
government and in private indus-
try, in accounting. Her hobbies
include singing, writing poetry,
knitting, and dog-sitting.

## The Meadow

The summer-child, pausing in the
August sun and beckoning
to me now, still laughs with joy
even in the advancing days
of the late December snows—

She waits for me as I drift in reverie . . .
turning from the shimmering brook
where I watch the minnows swim
and glancing back towards
swaying fronds of the weeping willow tree,
I run and play across the green meadow,
immersed in my radiant summer haven—

This is where my joy began
then turned to sheer delight—
nor will its rapture ever leave
that quiet corner of my heart—

## Playmates

I love your winds, Lord,
whipping up the green and golden
elm leaves of mid-November—
sweeping around me
with a cool and soothing touch—
moving the clouds
of grey like a cape billowing
across the heavens—
whirring through the branches
of the bronze and yellow maples,
twirling me around
as if to lift me high
to frolic with
scarlet treasures falling
from an autumn sky—

*Josephine Darner*

A native of Washington, D.C., has
worked in the theater as both a
dancer and an actress and still
enjoys taking dance classes. This is
her tenth appearance in *The Poet's
Domain*. ROAD Publishers has
published two books of Ms.
Darner's poetry, *The Music of
Memories* in 1995 and *The Dance
Within* in 1999. Ms. Darner is a
member of The National League
of American Pen Women, where
she serves as vice president of the
Bethesda Chapter. She lives in
Rockville, Md., where she contin-
ues to write poetry and also likes to
participate in local poetry readings.

Josephine Darner

# The Garden

In the early mornings I pull
Open the white wooden gate
And wade through long grass
Wet with dew around my feet—
I stand immersed in my grandmother's
Garden as if I were a part of
The floral harvest—
Monarch butterflies inspect my
Flowered dress, then arc away to
Graze on rainbowed zinnias—

The mornings seem to sing as if
All the world were as enchanted
As the vivid circle of my garden company—
Spider webs still laced with dew are
Curtains on castle windows and the
Blue larkspurs are tall delicate princesses—
Hovering above me, wings of yellow swallowtails
Catch the rays of the morning sun—

I dare to move—slowly drawing close to
The elegant white dahlias, then turning to
Gaze at the mystery of dark red gladiolas—
I am mesmerized—
Surely this is my earthly paradise—

Josephine Darner

## The Flower

The shadow-child, sleeping such a
long while in a cradle of time,
was floating heavy-lidded in the sea of
my unconscious mind—

A seed of sorrow lay rooted in her heart
as if that identity was formed
years before, bringing forth a
phantom harbored
in solitude like a

Lotus bud borne on a smooth, silent pool—

Then coaxed awake by small tokens of love
sent her way she stretched,
slowly unfolding like the

Lotus blossoming amidst nothing known
save the heart's hidden longing—

Now, skipping as if through
the winsome gate of youth,
I find a new flower emerging and
I am joyously transformed—

## Memories of Myself

Struggling to find a way
To understand my self
My mirror, broken to pieces
Shattered, cracked, and tattered by age
By memories
Places I can be my true self
Hiding my true wants
My true tears
Cascading down my pale skin
Reaching deep down to my heart
Forcing me to be something I am not
Fake in every memory, fake in every way
Will I ever be able to show those true colors?
Those true colors of mine

*Amanda Diehr*

lives in Charlottesville, Va. and is a college student pursuing a liberal arts degree. She hopes to graduate in the fall of 2006. Cars, reading, and writing poetry are her chief hobbies.

## Within Myself

Darkened shadows haunt my soul
Concealing my life without losing control
Lifting my gaze up above this loss
To see the light and future ahead
Only dreams can behold
A mesmerism, an ambition
To become something.
The reflection stares back at me
Alone inside the constraints of this skin
Not looking past to see what's within
Making an everlasting impression
To regard this self
As not just another.

Jean Doing

Active member of Writer's Center in Bethesda where she won a scholarship. Graduate of College of William and Mary. Retired human resources business executive, working part-time as director of a nonprofit that provides job counseling for people fifty-five and older. Published in *Scribble* publication of Maryland Writers' Association and *Lit Wit*, a periodical published in Metropolitan Washington, D.C. Selected two times (2004 and 2005) to have poems hung in Montgomery County Executive's *Poetry Gallery*. Working to publish chapbooks currently.

## In Praise of Child's Play

As a seven-year-old I danced
and giggled with other kids in July
in the magical circle
of the lawn sprinkler.
We cavorted in every direction
beneath the watery arch.
Our boisterous celebration caused
a peaceful spider web to tremble
where it stretched above the summer roses.

Blissfully aware that
this was our time and place,
we crowed our pleasure at the rainbow colors
of cloud-nine summer days,
energy up, senses alive.
Happiness bubbled up through our voices
and spilled across the flower beds
making a joyful noise.

## Breakfast Food

The inside panel of the cereal box
has a printed message:
"Sorry, you are not an instant winner,
please try again."
Smiling, I tilt the carton,
wheat flakes rustle from the paper liner
into my cereal bowl.
I add blueberries, sugar, milk
and pick up a spoon.

The instant winner would skip breakfast,
turn cartwheels, phone
everybody she knows,
and wake up the entire family.
The instant winner would plan a new life,
contact a broker, call a travel agent,
adopt a charity, all in one morning.

Jean Doing

My spoon uncovers the blue stenciled rose
centered in the bottom of the bowl.
I linger only a moment,
for I have things to do today;
I must drop off the dry cleaning,
I will pay the utilities,
struggle with a quarterly budget,
wrap a present, get a haircut—
a list not related to dreams.

Still the house is serenely quiet.
Nobody else has stirred.
I move quickly to the pantry
pull down a fresh box of cereal
and tear back the top.

## Reassured

This morning
when I stretched
my garden trowel
from kneeling bench
to damp April soil
and placed a new hydrangea
tentatively upright,
I smiled a toddler's
first-step victory grin.

## The Poet and the Whale

After recording whales
in multi-tonal conversations
and melodious underwater rumbling
a marine biologist states
that the majestic mammals
do not report the news
don't gossip about daily living
or quote Hamlet
and the Gettysburg address.
Whales speak of abstract things
trying to convey

Jean Doing

the rolling beauty around them.
I feel connected
to these mighty creatures.
Both of us struggle to tell
what has washed into our hearts
from the murky ocean
of our lives,
my verses, a light contrast
to the thunderous shading
of their trumpeting songs.

## The Rescue

November allows warm afternoons
where sun smoothes out
early morning sharp edges
of days that move past Thanksgiving
to the cold sting of winter.

In the garden
a stark white geranium cluster
hugs low, dark green leaves
holding its open face high
in the sunshine.

This flower will be gone
with another frost
its vibrant blossom too perfect
to die as a faded reminder
of summer past.

Leaning down I clip the geranium head
taking it to the kitchen with me.
In a tumbler of water
on the window sill
it stands proudly
saluting the promise
of flowers next spring.

## Roethke: Crazy Like a Fox

Otto's little boy clambered or dropped
to the greenhouse roof, delved in mud
at the shaded drainage ditch, named the nameless
creatures there, precociously, sprinkled them
like passwords in his rhymes to dazzle
assistant editors opening the mail, noses tickling.

Year by year he approached, coyly rhyming.
Stepping lightly away from the lawyer career
left over from another generation's dream . . .
A lawyer! inhabiting adulthood forever, shunning
the ever-blooming roses, the refuge of madness?
His laughter rang out, undraftable at last.

Did he let his hair grow? Was he restless, taciturn,
ebullient by turns? Did his students matter?
More than a few? And what of the faculty,
mentors, supporters, probers, and partners
in his North Pacific nest. His wife, ah yes.
Fame. Was that what he wanted? He moved
        among giants.

The manuscript that would have been his next,
turned out to be the last, just fooling with the
        stops,
trying out a shocker, flashing a skillful blade,
still faithful to the cult of naming-magic as of old,
and titles might or might not mystify.
Some older themes returned, in a doubtful tone.

From first to last he bled his vein of memory,
carelessly free as a goat on its rock,
looking back at me, shouting "Dare!"
        This is for every human alive:
        To give tongue, in chorus or alone,
        To dance in costume of the day.

*Rosemary Dolgner*

Since her work appeared in the
1995 and 1996 volumes of *The
Poet's Domain*, Rosemary has
studied Theatre Arts at Lynchburg
College for a second bachelor's
degree. For a couple of years she
produced computer layout for the
quarterly editions of *The Potomac
Review*. Her poems have been
published in *Grandmother Earth
IV, Common Threads*, Spring–
Summer 1999; and in *The Comstock
Review*, Spring–Summer 2001.

## The People Are Gone

We call them the ancient ones.
We tiptoe quietly past the ruins
   of their cliff-top houses,
   on paths created by their sandals.
We see bits and pieces of their lives,
   in pottery shards
   and scraps of woven cloth.
We feel their souls in drawings
   on crumbling walls,
   magical sketches of animals and people.
In the rocks, they have left us
   their stories of life and joy and death.
A smudged handprint on a cave wall
   reaches out to connect,
   beyond time and place.
We are here, because they came first.
They are our family, our yesterday.

*Sharon Dorsey*

(b.1943, Charmco, W. Va.) has been freelancing with fiction, non-fiction, juvenile fiction, and poetry for many years. Her work has appeared in *McCalls, Christian Singles, The Colonial Williamsburg News, Expats International, Mature Living, Together, Ashland Oil Newsletter, The Beacon,* and the *Journal of the Glen Canyon Institute.* She has three times been awarded 3rd place, Juvenile Fiction, as well as 3rd place and 1st place, Non-Fiction, at the CNU Writers' Conference. Sharon shares her love of writing with her daughter Shannon whose work also appears in this publication.

Sharon Dorsey

## Journeys

The ghosts of vacation past are walking with me.
My serenity and confidence are disturbed.
I'm stepping in my own footprints through
    fairy castles and fragrant rose gardens.
Everything's the same . . .
Smiling couples, everywhere, couples, coax
    reluctant toddlers on the carousel.
The aroma of popcorn and cotton candy tan-
    talizes the senses.
Everything's the same, yet, nothing's the same.
My toddler is a tall, straight teen.
I walk alone now, in my old footprints, but I
    am not the same.
The old me waited for someone to take her
    hand and lead her to happiness.
The new me strides through unexplored terri-
    tory in search of her own rainbow.
The old me feared change.
The new me welcomes it, embraces it.
The old me leaned.
The new me can allow others to lean.
The old me needed to take and take.
The new me has more to give.
The old ghosts can sleep in peace without regrets,
While the new spirits of joy and freedom fill
    the empty footprints and stride ahead.

## Cabbage Worm

The spring sun
woke up my mother,
sleeping, in her cocoon.
She did not see her beauty.
She did not know the miracle.
Three hundred eggs she put
under the new green fronds
for the Lepidoptera life.
I was born in this cabbage.
It is my bed and my food
and my home.
I am velvet green
with rays on my back,
eyes, half blind, and surrounded by green
six legs to march and
ten stumps to cling to my leafy ground.
I stretch my caterpillar body
to grasp the next mouthful,
my job, my recreation, my game.
I curl myself inside the cool shadows
against the birds.
When it is my time
I begin to knit
the walls of my own cocoon.
My dark dormitory.
I don't understand why.
I sleep.
I wait.
I change.
I don't understand the miracle.
And yet in the spring
I am as she.
White wings opened.
I go to fly
along the rows
of cabbages.

*Suzanne E. Dundon*

is a psychiatrist, wife, mother, and perpetual explorer of the rooms and passageways of the infinite mind.

Suzanne E. Dundon

## There He Was

There he went, again,
and despite the cold,
naked, on the beach,
stood tall and strong
as a tree,
unflinching in the test of the bitter wind,
unbowed,
rooted upon the sandy shore
which held him there
as if to conquer the arrogant tide
and breaking waves.
Look on me,
he seemed to say,
I am a man.

## Aura

Eyes like those are scarce.
They throw off a brightness
that steams up the vision
in the mirror of your old life.
Her outlines are frayed.
They sway in the light of your match.
Your fingertips rub
the lace at her waist.
Thoughts swarm in your head.
You are charmed—
without pretense.
Bewilderment gnaws at you.
You mutter your desire,
with shame of your greed,
for her.
Before today,
women were trinkets
and you, running around and panting,
finally, became too annoyed
with their crumbs and crusts
of love.

*Suzanne E. Dundon*

Now, you have come here
to this house, this chair, this bed
to edit your life and
to verify, blindly,
furtively,
your faith in green eyes,
that flow and foam
like the waves of the deep sea.

## Among the Half-dead Trees

Among the half-dead trees
I wandered to your high fence
Which kept me out,
Raised above the dull brown meadow.

Beside the dry riverbed,
I saw your mill inside
That ground golden flour,
And water that flowed like silver mirrors
From the depths of the earth.

Near the ancient brick wall
Still warm from your sun,
I rested my sheep
And heard your laugh from afar.

Later, you told me of a day of pure beauty,
Of trees so alive,
Of sheep white as snow,
Of rocks uncovered in the river,
Etched with fossils,
And a longing to go walking in the pasture
Outside your high fence.

Suzanne E. Dundon

# Near This Rose, Another Woman
# Appeared Out of the Depths of My Being

I am an ant
That travels over the pink petals.
I am a ray of light
That caresses the transparent curves.
I am a bee
That seeks the sweet deep center.
I am an eye
That is captivated by single leaf.
I am a camera
That memorizes the fleeting beauty.
I am a supplicant
That kneels in front of this gift.
I am an admirer, a secret lover, a helper, a sister.

I was one woman.
Another woman I am.

I was
A rose.
Now I am she who beholds the beauty
And sees in front of me
A new sweet field of roses.

## Emerging

The cocoon slips away
I am poised
breath retained
in the delicate balance
exquisite bliss
vast emptiness.
Not yet time to fly.

## The Fruit Tree

Pruned
new buds swell
drinking in
abiding
confident
leaves will come
and provide
perfect nourishment
for concentric circles
of annual growth
sustained by heartwood
Fruit, sweet and juicy
is inevitable

*Janet Evergreen*

(b.1956) first lived at 4 Pig Rock Lane, Marblehead, Mass. Her spiritual path is supported by Tibetan Buddhist Drikung Kagyu practice and her main deity is Pigheaded Vajrayogini. Her work is to be a spiritual friend and guide, mainly through Cranial Sacral manipulation and Body Centered Spiritual Processing, not unlike loosening—or is it losing—our marbles. Other adventures not foreseen by her birthplace include raising one biological daughter, two adopted sons, and dozens of foster kids before discovering her own inner child of luminous light who simply enjoys life in Charlottesville, Virginia.

Janet Evergreen

## Spring Rejoicing

Like a snake
I have shed my skin
underneath opens to luminous space

Like a tree
my roots have gone deeper
quiescent buds of compassion swell

Like a butterfly
I am emerging
wings wet with blessings

Patient, confident, resting,
little by little,
no hurry

My heart is
simply quietly
rejoicing

## Eden

The Garden never was the Paradise
we'd hoped it was so many years ago;
The promises demanded too much sacrifice.
The Garden never was the Paradise
we'd hoped . . .
     seemed more a hope for melting ice.
What beauty ever warmed the heart of Iago?
The Garden never was the Paradise
we'd hoped it was so many years ago.

## Leaves Falling

Pete Freas

(b.1942, Cleveland, Ohio) retired
Navy helicopter pilot (26 years,
Vietnam Vet), retired Virginia
teacher, early Social Security
retiree. Poet since grade 8; pub-
lished two chapbooks; founded
Chesapeake Bay Poets where he
publishes A LINE IN TIME (a
weekly online poetry newsletter);
maintains a poetry web site (ches-
baypoets.org); and edits *Skipping
Stones*, an annual anthology of
Hampton Roads poets and artists.
    He is working on two poetry
books, two novels, and a verse
drama. Pete is married with an
adult son and daughter (twins).

Spring leaves falling
sadden me. Every
breath of wind
shakes green confetti
from the trees.
It doesn't seem
we'll lose the
trees—they sport
new foliage daily.
Still, it is
unnatural they're falling
now, their soft
green faces glistening
with tears, eyes
young, afraid. I
want to rake
them up, burn
them before they
are dry, gray
feathers scattered, forgotten.

Pete Freas

# Nomads

Before millennia, we were travelers
following the seasons, following the herds.
Getting on was always hard-scrabble;
in sickness and in health, we had to move or die.
One day someone somewhere, some way,
learned to tame the food
we'd always wandered after. Then,
we started building fences;
huts and walls began displacing tents;
we became enclaves and called
ourselves civilized. Back then,
we had to shout across the wind
on horseback to survive; at night
we talked in quiet tones and sometimes
smoked or chewed. Always, we ate.
Now, our conversations are but motes
settled on convenience anywhere.
We shout at one another now so we
don't have to hear. No one listens.
We have to tear the fences down,
the huts and monuments and walls.
We don't need place or property.
We must have space and movement,
community of family and clan on horseback
following the seasons and the herds.
It's time Nomads took the world back.

Pete Freas

# Emmett

after hearing Nikki Giavonni
speak of Rosa Parks and Emmet Till

If a boy falls in the woods
and no kin is there to hear,
did it never happen?

What happens to the terror?

If a boy bleeds in the woods,
do the mocking birds
carry his cries to his home?

Do the trees weep for him?

If a boy dies in the woods
and no heart can hear,
does even the wind deny?

Where does the horror go?

Does the battered water of a creek
baptize wounds and cleanse
the soul of once a boy?

Do all the tears just disappear?

If a heart breaks in the woods,
will the forest be untouched?
Do even trees keep silence?

What happens to a mother's heart?

If the box lies open in the parlor,
will suffering wail from the tomb
and outrage beat its breast?

If not the forest, will not the streets cry out
their heartache and their rage?

Pete Freas

## Stargazer

I've wandered with the ancient mariners,
pursued the Northern Star
and Southern Cross;
I've battled men and gods alongside Mars
and blazed across the Milky Way. I've lost
my way and found myself among the stars
of Virgo, slept with Aphrodite, tossed
my fortune to the skies in hope that I
might find my way once more
to Eastern shores
whose sunrise paintbrush splashes 'cross the sky
bright hues and subtle shades that thrill me more
than visiting the constellations I
have trod upon a thousand years before
I found in vibrant pink this soothing grace,
with stamen gold, and white-rimmed petal face.

## In the Company of Poets

The threadbare jeans
and coffee-stained pullover
proclaim my profession
as much as the dancing pen
and pad of foolscap.

The pennies in my pocket
are never enough for a tip,
so I arrange them by my saucer
in connect-the-dot portraits
to entertain the waitress.

She'll understand. I've seen her
scribbling stanzas on the backs
of order tickets, pink tongue tip jutting
from the corner of her mouth
while she sifts words
for a golden phrase
to flawlessly describe—

—the woman sitting by the door
tearing perfume samples
from a magazine,
swiping them on her wrists

—her friend, who teases that
she'll have to rub her arms
beneath her husband's nose
before he'll notice

—or, perhaps, me,
sitting here
searching for a way
to describe her.

*Bill Glose*

is an award-winning writer whose prose and poetry have appeared in *GRIT, Red River Press, The Summerset Review,* and numerous other markets. Glose's honors include the 2001 F. Scott Fitzgerald Short Story Award, and a 2004 Virginia Press Association award. When he is not writing his regular column for *Virginia Living* or poetry for himself, Glose can be found photographing nature landscapes on Virginia's Peninsula. More information is available online at www.BillGlose.com.

Bill Glose

# A Lesson From My Dogs

When I encounter
well-meaning friends
who boast of their success,
offer career advice, suggest
alternatives to writing,
I ask my dogs,
the reasons why.

"Do you ever worry," I say,
"what other dogs think, wonder
which ones growl behind
your back? Do you crave
better chew toys, designer food
from a can? Ever wish
you were something else?"

They pant and wag until
I snap their leashes on
and open the door, then
they sprint outside,
towing me behind.

There's a whiff of something
on the breeze
and they must investigate,
sniff and run,
be what they were meant to be.

## In the Box

At our fiftieth college reunion,
we try to stuff each other
back in the box that once contained us.
But some that were beauty queens
now look like Grandma Moses paintings.
Some who were dowdy now have style.
The box has many doors and windows.

On the stage of the vacant recital hall,
we five friends watch our ex-roommate's fingers
glide magically through Bach's Goldberg
Variations.
We hear no difference in her faultless fashioning
of time and intonation.
All is well until it is my turn to sing.

I go to stand in front of the excellent Steinway,
passing the offending box.
"Me, me, me, me, me," I quip,
the comedian's warm-up,
indicating my abdication
from the world of music.

"But you must sing," they say.
And so I flutter in and out of
a new song about being borne up on Eagle's
wings.
The box, looming large on the steps,
shivers as I do, as my friends frown gently
and look away,

Later that evening, they will discover
what I know I have become
as I hold my book,
the one that bears my name.
I read to them from the words I have written,
words that have made me what I am.
My five friends smile.

*Doris Gwaltney*

is the author of *Shakespeare's Sister, George Purdie, Merchant of Smithfield,* and *Duncan Browdie, Gent.* She has published short fiction and poetry in the *Greensboro Review, The Poet's Domain, The Beacon, The William and Mary Review, Virginia Adversaria, Cube,* and *In Good Company.* She has given speeches and presented workshops at a number of colleges and at The Virginia Festival of the Book. She teaches a writing class for the Center for Community Learning at Christopher Newport University. Her most recent work, *Homefront,* a middle grade novel, is listed in the Simon & Schuster fall catalogue for 2005.

## The Osprey

You came every spring
to your home
(a penthouse on a pole in the river)
to repair/prepare the nest
for offspring to come.

It must have surprised
to see it gone,
nothing but the watery river.

The hurricane had greedily taken our dock
and your home as it galed by.

We loved to watch
the sweep of your wings
as you circled your bedraggled nest,
signaling the comfort and the surety
of spring.
They beat the warming air
as you busily refurbished your love nest,
for soon there would be
tiny heads poking up
sometimes two—sometimes three.

And you would do the feeding ritual
magnificently arcing to the water
then rising, clutching a silver fish
intact between your claws.
More skillful than any fisherman
I had ever seen.

You liked the neighborhood
so you stubbornly tried
to rebuild
on the cupola next to the river,
but gravity would have none of it.
We tried to help you anchor it.
It would not stay.

Claire M. Hasselbeck

After an early plunge into writing poetry, Claire set it aside for more practical ventures. Recently, she decided it was time to dig out some of her past work and to begin writing again. In 2003 she joined a weekly poetry group at the Osher Lifelong Learning Institute affiliated with George Mason University in Fairfax, Va. The weekly deadline and the excellent support of her fellow poets revived her passion for writing. Several of her poems were published in volume 21 of *The Poet's Domain*.

*Claire M. Hasselbeck*

So you went elsewhere
to live.

We miss your glorious announcement
of spring,
the constancy of your return,
your vigilant care for new life,
our time so well spent
contemplating your perfect illustration
of the circle/cycle of life.

## I Should Have Known

I really should have known.

My father with his pale skin
which reddened in the sun,
his blue, poetic eyes,
his hair—white, as long as I could remember.

The three of us—his children
with the same pale hue
which reddened with the sun,
a sniff of alcohol,
an embarrassing or awkward moment.

I should have known

When the gray streaked through my hair at
thirty
that by sixty—I'd be an apple on a stick.
Though slim in youth—never small of waist—
a slight inward curve there
where my girlfriends made hourglasses
with theirs.

I should have known.

My father's name never fit us,
we liked to joke and dance too much,
there was a tug at my heart at the color green,
I was baptized on the day itself—March 17<sup>th</sup>
An omen?

Claire M. Hasselbeck

I should have known

those moods of dark despair
came from a green gene in my soul.
and the gift of gab—when loosened with a sip
of scotch.

It finally came out at a wake—
Where else?

"Your grandfather (the map of Ireland on his
face) was adopted.
You're from THAT side of the family
McGillicuddy was your great grandfather."

I really should have known
From the old sod we were blown.


## The Man on the Grate

I pull myself from the tentacles of sleep,
push myself into the early morning air,
begin my jarring jog over sidewalks,

Past row houses snuggled up against each other.
One sighs deeply in its sleep,
exhaling a puff of smoke.

A mound of clothes on a grate stirs furtively
like a startled animal,
as I lurch by.

A human figure rises from the mound.
The old captain sits up,
his white beard foaming against his sea-
weathered face.

He stands to gaze at some distant ship
or approaching storm, ramrod straight
in heavy, navy blue, brass buttoned coat

*I've heard your family bought it for you.*
*You could live with them in luxury.*
*But you chose the grate—your ship,*
*your freedom.*

Claire M. Hasselbeck

I plod on
distracted from my sweaty journey,
curious about his—

His adventures,
his battles with the turbulent sea.

*I salute you and your final battle,*
*To live as you choose*
*Captain of the grate*
*Captain of your ship*
*Captain of your soul.*

## The Chapel

We have risen
from our bed
to celebrate
the rising of the dead.

My faith prefers
to lie slumbering
beneath a worn coverlet,
woven of years of tangled experiences.

The small chapel
simple and unpretentious
demands nothing of me.

It fills with the words, the music,
the choreography
of prayer.

Surrounding me with
peace
hope.

It is enough
to be there.

Claire M. Hasselbeck

# Joanna

Joanna singing in the kitchen,
As thin as a stalk of sugar cane,
Skin the color of warm, brown clay,
Peeling, stirring and chopping,
Swaying to the music of her own voice.

She worked all day to her song,
Then went home
To sleep
In her cardboard box.

When it rained,
She sang a song about rain.
It rained for days.
Joanna sang.

One night,
She went home
To her hillside.
Rain had washed her cardboard box away.

Joanna had nowhere to live,
So she came to live with us.
Slept on the floor
Of the tiny kitchen.
She woke the next day
To clean and cook
And sing.

## Hummingbird

When there is no more time and life is done,
take me to Heaven on a Hummer's wing!
This magic bird is chariot enough,
riding the trade winds for a thousand miles,
darting its way through ancient forest glens,
sipping its strength from tiny velvet blooms.
I want no marble mansions in the stars,
no golden gateways to ideal lands;
give me the scent of angels in a rose,
the quiet thunder of a distant storm—
Oh Earth, sweet Earth, in life so little seen,
What wonders are there waiting to be found
in just the rhythm of a single leaf!

## Daydreams

Now wouldn't it be grand if He is truly there?
If all our introspections, hopes and dreams
are duly noted by Whatever framed their
source?

Alas for Man—his universe has been too
spare
with love and truth and intellect and time;
and I'm so tired of public sentiment and song,

I long for something just to think to! So,
although I've pruned the rose and planted
marigolds today,
made stew and gingerbread and one small
rhyme to share,

oh, wouldn't it be grand if (for the private
thoughts)
Someone is there?

Barbara McKay Hewin

was born in New York City in 1927. She was educated in art and history at Ohio State University and The George Washington University and received her B.A. with honors at Christopher Newport University. Married 56 years and living in Newport News and Williamsburg, Virginia, she and her husband, Larry, have two children and one grandchild. She has participated in many civic activities, which included costuming many local opera and theater productions. She has won awards for her poetry, and her poems have appeared in volumes 1 through 21 of *The Poet's Domain*.

Barbara McKay Hewin

## The Child

Dear Child of Love, the open passion from
a brilliant moment brought you into being;
inside my womb the roundness of you formed,
and filled my soul with dreams of love to
come!
How good it was to know you live and stirring,
for never was there pain or doubt or fearing,
I ate and slept with quiet tender sharing,
the pressure of you held to me uncaring.
I walked with firmer step and faith affirmed.

Then when you came, the sight of your dear eyes
so wide and new and full of bright surprise
brought sweeter joy than I had ever known.
The downy press of your pale helpless frame
was such a weight as I will ever prize;
recalled when anger grips an aching nerve,
upheld again when grieving dulls the same,
when you are tall and confidently grown,
that charming golden day will still arise.

In joy conceived, conceiving joyous days,
you added to my life unbounded worth:
the happy smile, the chubby clinging hand,
the sleepy kiss, the weeping from the heart,
the patient faith, the unrestrained mirth—
no matter what God does in future ways,
reflections of your childhood and my love
will ever credit all that He has planned,
will ever hold a mirror to His art.

Barbara McKay Hewin

## September Sail

The seas are gray today
and autumn tints the air with brine,
and butterflies above our wake low fly
till one by one they fall beneath its foam and
die.
Trees on the shore away
beyond—red-brown and green—combine
their shades gray-blended with the sea and sky.
While sailing the horizon's line, white sails go
by.

And so we anchor, soft,
the wavelets chatter by the bow;
the gulls fly near, and through the misty
shrouds
their fervent calls create a natural harmony.
The clouds are slow aloft;
I write with magic ease somehow,
for like the butterflies, gone are the crowds,
and God may see His world new ways today
through me.

## I Rejoice in Haiku

Left Bank denizen
In Paris I rejoiced in
Being what I was.

Back beyond the pale
In Erin I rejoiced in
Being what I was.

Upper East Sider
In New York I rejoiced in
Being what I was.

Irish ceili dancer
In Jersey I rejoiced in
Being what I was.

*William L. Hickey*

(b.1929, Baltimore, Md.) was an information analyst and writer for the National Council on Crime and Delinquency. He does square, round, and Irish ceili dancing. His poems have appeared in volumes 17 through 20 of *The Poet's Domain*, and an Anthology of the Poetry Society of Virginia, *The Oak*, and are forthcoming in *The Lantern* (Galway, Ireland). He lives to dance and write in Virginia Beach, Va.

## The Five Houses of Stone

Mahalia and Ethel built their houses with rocks
that the waters would never sweep away.
How great their art
expressed their inward soul
while keeping their spirits strong
with voices vibrato deep
singing the gospel's
promised goal.

Thanks to both of you
we on this earth still plod on;
unimpressed by human frailty and greed,
you lifted us up towards the heavens
and the love we really need.

And here's to you, Billie,
your message will not be forgot;
your raspy voice raised our consciousness
to strange fruit and the hangman's knot.

And to you, Lena, you taught us to be proud
that all our bodies are beautiful
and to endure the stormy weather
not surrendering to darkening clouds.

And finally to you, Aretha,
who filled our hearts
with joy and laughter
bringing us the respect
we all do hunger after.

*Todd Hubley*

(b.1943, Louisville, Ky.) lives an
active life as a husband, researcher,
writer, poet, part-time amateur
actor and singer, dramatist, and
director of company plays, and is
making his eighth appearance in
*The Poet's Domain*. His poem
*Sunshine and Shadow* was includ-
ed in the International Library of
Poetry's *America at the
Millennium: The Best Poems and
Poets of the 20th Century*, pub-
lished in 2000, and he qualified as
a semifinalist for his poem, *The
Storm* at the 1998 International
Society of Poets' annual conven-
tion held in Washington, D.C.

## Among the Half-dead Trees

I wander
thinking of the dormant life
the nutritious earth
I amend by hand
the leaves, the bark, the mulch of pine
the pine cones the fruit of the conifer
the rotted branches and everything organic
become earth, blood for the spring.
Among the half-dead trees
I make a canvas from the Creator
soon there will be green
there will be white in the night
the snakes, the bees
the butterflys, the grasshoppers
all will have habitat
there will be moss and lichen
where the light never touches
and the new trees will mature
for protecting the foliage in bloom.

Matt Inderlied

Virginia Beach, Va. is home for me now. In my free time I enjoy many things: my family and friends and dog Dulcinea and girlfriend and beach and woods and guitar and *Don Quijote*. I have been reading *Don Quijote* for a long time now. I teach Spanish and have a small business. I enjoy writing poetry in Spanish. I think it makes my English sound better. I have a garden. It's a small woodland garden. I love Mother Nature. I watch little TV. When I do, it's *Fox News* or bull riding. I'm interested in our world and in life in general.

Matt Inderlied

## Near That Rose

She was sown a rose of simplicity
from the depths of her being
she endured a season
until one day like passion
she left the seedling white
lonely among other lovers of the garden
she was a virgin in waiting

Then he was sown a rugosa rose
from the depths of his being
he matured a season
until one passionate day
he left the seedling red
he breathed a new life

Their will was one
entwined they made love
they never separated again
they were of the same root
they were of the same breath

## Who's Rejoicing?

Nobody's rejoicing in his being what he is
Mean ole man, always has been.
Younger, he was meaner still,
What gives him the right
To be so ornery and cantankerous?
She ought to know,
'Been with him all these years.
Did they ever have a really nice day?
Alone, maybe, but not together.
How can they stay in the same house?
Miserable with, miserable without,
S'pose she understands him.
And maybe in those earlier years
When they were very young,
They did love each other
And shared their dreams.
He is what he is . . .
And she is still holding on.

*Beverley Isaksen*

Writing poetry has been a part of my life since the second grade. Poetry and theatre combine to give me a way to express my experiences in life. I am a Norfolk native, married for sixty-one years to a naval aviator. We are now retired and recently returned to Norfolk after some fifty years away and it is nice to be home. Four score years have given me many poems and more to come. But when I have to leave this mortal coil, I know I shall say, "Just a minute, I haven't finished writing!" Or, "Can you come back later?"

## Missed Appointment

There's a haunting in my mind
And time is fine tuning the spectre.
It is ahead of me or behind me—
And each day stretches like elastic
To make itself another day.
Time is a genius, a specialist in corruption
Of my well-planned structures,
Splintering into other times.
Memory and reality
Double back on each other.
It matters that I'm a week ahead
Or a week behind
I'm losing control. . . .
Is it me I hear laughing?

Beverley Isaksen

## Do I Really Know Who I Am?

So long I have wondered
Now I know—I am a misplaced person.
Things around me are dissonant and strange,
I seem to belong in another time, another century.
I cannot imagine how it happened. . . .
Someone else's skin encloses me—
I don't think I can give it back.
All right, I will accept this body
But my mind is what
I really want to keep as me
My ideals for this space I occupy
Stay with me, hopefully to nourish changes
And foster respect one for another.
Oh, I enjoy being who I am—
Born to play the part of a thorn.
My convictions cause a lot of laughter
And disagreement when I speak
Of how I wish we would present ourselves.
Ah well, this old body
May not last long enough
To see my young friends become misplaced, too.

## Weather Report

The soles of my feet hit the carpet
as I swing out of bed,
last night's weather forecast
tickling inside my head.
I run to the window. Yes!
Snowfall has begun;
I'll have to shovel my walk.
I will have to cancel my plans for the day.
How inconvenient! How wonderful!
I turn away from the window,
do a little snow dance
and I am once again eight years old.

Nancy Bayliff Jarvis

(b.1932, Annapolis, Md.) Nancy was married to a career military man for 30 years and was a stay-at-home mom with four children. When the children were grown, she worked as a floral designer for five years, then entered civil service, working for the National Technical Information Service for twenty years. Since retirement in 2001, she has been attending classes at the Osher Lifelong Learning Institute, affiliated with George Mason University. She enjoys the variety of classes, which range from poetry, music, and literature to current events and history.

## Dancing

This may be the last dance.
Come, take a chance and waltz with me.
There's much to learn and more to see.
As we step to the music our eager minds hear:
Aging and time are nothing to fear.

## A Poet's Poem

A poem can be a simple thing:
words that have a truthful ring
Drop some words on that page
Free those words from their cage
In your mind they spin around
Catch them if you like their sound.

## A Backward Look Inside

As a child, I often prayed for power
to ease family quarrels and disappointments,
to erase the frownings and sad looks of hurt,
sensing the first healing smile must be my own!
Beginning peacemakers must first learn peace.

As a new wife, the rule of smiling first
was often forced, camouflaging tears
provoked by a live-in mother-in-law—
dependent feelings blotched her lovingness.
Beginning marriage exacts diplomacy.

As a new mother, my stage-struck dreams
came true imitating serenity my mom
always had, showing no fear, no ineptness,
collapsing only when no one was near!
Beginning mothers follow childhood dreams.

As a senior citizen, I haven't lost
my smile, serenity, or tact—entirely!
Now, simple things seem wearily uphill
and something new can make me come undone.
What should I begin? Starting over again?

A backward look at me brings contemplation
of other women's dreams, their search for peace,
their uphill climbs that brought a new exult!
Their sorrows and their griefs bring understanding;
they're much like me—in that I do rejoice!

*Rosalie S. Jennings*

(b.1917, Woodstock, Va.) is a member of the Valley Branch of Virginia National League of American Pen Women. She has recently had eight of her poems depicted by an artist displayed in a local showing. Her 1999 illustrated chapbook *Leaning On Rhythms* has been well received, and is on display in local libraries and in the Washington, D.C., League of American Pen Women library.

Rosalie S. Jennings

## From the Floor

Flying redbirds, compelled to soar
By the power of panting gusts,
Leave me rooted to this forest floor,
Here in the stir of leafy dust.

Ricocheting from restless air,
Strong current skims a swaying tree,
Then glances off her yellow hair
To lift my own, caressing me.

Part of me climbs the streaks of light,
Part of me stays near the rooted tree,
Part of me wishes for greater height,
All of me wants to be safe, but free!

# A+

Archaic, Arthritic
Asthmatic, Absurd
Advisor, Amusing
Ancestor, Alert

Always Amazing
Antique, Alive
Ancient, Awesome
Ambitious, Abrupt

Accommodating
Appreciated, Artistic
Assured, Animated
Absent-minded, too!

When all is said and done,
My name is *Grandma*!

*Barbara Daniels Johnson*

(b.1928, Cleveland, Ohio) has
lived in the Alexandria, Va. area
since 1934. She has three daugh-
ters and one grandson. Interests
include church, crafts, and chil-
dren. She is active in senior choir
and Vacation Bible School. She is
recording secretary, Alexandria
Branch, National League of
American Pen Women, and a
member of its Poetry Workshop.
She authored *Shared Happiness*, a
book of poetry.

## Saturn's Moon

"Enceladus, the 6th largest of Saturn's known moons,
is one of the most reflective objects in the solar sys-
tem. It rebounds nearly all visible light that hits it. It
is so reflective that scientists believe there must be
frozen water in its atmosphere. The moon's gravity
isn't sufficient to hold an atmosphere for very long,
so there must be a strong continuous source of
geysers, volcanic activity or gases seeping from the
interior." *Virginian-Pilot,* Saturday, March 19, 2005

Paula Lippard Justice Ph.D.

has been an educator in Hampton
Roads for many years. She is cur-
rently an assistant professor in com-
munication at Old Dominion
University, a practising licensed
professional counselor in Virginia
Beach, and a recorded minister in
the religious society of Friends
(Quakers) in the Virginia Beach
Friends Meeting. She loves the arts
in all forms, writes poetry, draws,
and acts in an improvisational
theater, Playback Hampton Roads.

My name is Enceladus and mine a cautionary tale.
Enceladus, one of old Saturn's concubines,
I spin a cruel circle round my dark master
whose love still draws me in,
I, a pale ghost, and he my lost
and weary warrior
who could not save himself or me.

I come to warn you, blue planet,
third from the Sun,
warn you of the withering of the green life,
the browning of grasslands, the wasting of
sweet waters
until your great round heart
shrivels like ripe fruit in desert heat.
He was once like you, a lush young god
blood red and ebony soil, veined with purple ore,
a proud passion throbbing deep in his core.
And I, Enceladus, soft and moving,
awash in silver waters
danced with him in the Sun.
Reckless in his immortality, he spent our youth
in plunder, war and magic,
and in our age, empty,
we were cast into outer darkness.

Now old and sere,
I turn a cold face toward the distant Sun,
my only mourning reflection,

Paula Lippard Justice

My frozen longing mirroring a billion tears of
Light across the galaxies
while beneath my icy surface, deep rivers of
rage and grief turn to air and fire.
I turn and turn again on a hard and bitter
path, beaten down and barren
where no tender living thing will ever push its
way through darkness
singing my name softly.

But I am a portent goddess, sweet fresh God,
foreshadowing your end.
Remember us, the foolish old Man and his
beautiful dreamer,
Remember the fire that fed our passion and
now feeds yours
is none of your own.
And if you are not wise in how you use that
time in the Sun,
the measure of light you are given,
its fire will purify your soul.

## Rose

Sweet the rose,
slender bud in slender glass,
sweet, sweet its scent
    on my table.
Yellow shading into saffron,
delicate petals unfurling,
each day changing.

Unable—unable to let it go,
I watched full-blown glory
fade, dry, and brown—
to find its scent deeper,
sweeter now!

*Carrie Jackson Karegeannes*

(b.1923, Wusih, China)— retired
editor and writer for newspapers, a
research corporation, and three
government agencies—has
appeared in 15 previous volumes
of *The Poet's Domain* as well as in
*Midwest Poetry Review, The
Pegasus Review, The Begonian,
Poetic Voices of America*, and other
journals and anthologies. A mem-
ber of the National League of
American Pen Women, Poetry
Society of Virginia, and Academy
of American Poets, she lives in
Falls Church, Va., after periods in
China, France, and Greece.

## Walking

Half moon in the softening sky
and fireflies in the grass
as evening comes.
Roses lift rich color, fragrance
along the path as I pass.

Pale old-fashion pink,
opening bud of velvet red,
"Tropicana's" brilliant tangerine,
a fluffy full-blown white—

wafting balm upon the air,
blessings on me, on all the night.

Carrie Jackson Karegeannes

## All New

Again all new!
All as imagined—
yet never imagined,
not believed.

Spring comes, new!
Again, unbelievably, green closes in,
fragrance, flowers, birdsong
of other years, incessant,
        remembered,
yet new.

Poignant with other springs,
yet like no other.
All new!

## Virginia October

Clouds of gold, copper, saffron—
and there a flash of scarlet—
engulf my world.
Flecks of yellow, of crimson, drift,
turning, shimmering, across the day,
perfection of maple leaf, sycamore,
        oak leaf
at my feet.

Not lost, not lost,
leaves, dreams, days drifting
        in sun,
nothing is lost.

# Flying

Though exhausted, I laugh.
After nine laps around the track
Coach tells me who he is.
Earlier Coach told me to follow
That little fellow over there as
He would set a good pace for me.
I followed him first lap, then watched
His little round behind get farther
And farther ahead until I heard him
Running behind me the eighth lap,
Saw him pass me on the ninth.
Freshman track is discouraging.

"Jeeze, he is good, Coach."
"Yeah, he was on the Olympic team."
"What!" I laugh but at the same
Time my back straightens as I
Rise to full height remembering
With exaltation that first
Lap: running with just three toe
Cleats biting the ground, wind
In my ears, flying around
The track with an Olympian!

# The Twinkling of an Eye

Love, a sea of love, overwhelms me,
Peace, unfathomable peace, fills my heart,
As I surrender, capitulate to the
Almightiness of the ground of my being
Here in this wilderness retreat.
His hands, gently laid on my head,
Could be those of any person
But these are Rob's, my Priest's, hands.
I hear him beseeching the Holy Spirit
To dwell in me, to fill me.
In the twinkling of an eye I am
Changed, though still brother, husband,
Father of four boys, doting grandpa.

Robert L. Kelly

began writing poetry as a student of Christine Sparks through the Lifelong Learning Society at Christopher Newport University. He continued with Mary-Jean Lanehart and now studies with Patricia Flower Vermillion at the university. He belongs to the Poetry Society of Virginia, serves on the advisory board of the Annual Christopher Newport University's Writers' Conference and revels in the large body of active, energetic, and exciting poets living in Hampton Roads.

Robert L. Kelly

## Apogee of My Trajectory

At the apogee of my trajectory,
high over the swimming pool,
in a second of weightlessness,
I am elated, fulfilled.

That missile flying down the range,
landing in the "pickle barrel,"
launched this morning by my young men
consecrated our long work together.

Being ejected from the sleeper into
New London darkness at 5:38am, Monday
after Monday, then heading for Electric
Boat Company had been worth doing.

These young officers of SSBN George
Washington were there waiting for
their "man from Washington" to keep
the Polaris test program on track.

Today at Cape Canaveral, they launched
the second Polaris missile ever fired
from a submarine veiled by the ocean depths.
It was perfect. Now we are celebrating.

Sitting beside the Satellite Motel
pool I am laughing as the Weapons
Officer is picked up and hurled into
the water followed by the Assistant

Weapons Officer, not expecting I
would be given, "1," "2," "3," "4,"
"5" to get my shoes and watch
off before being seized and

swung to the chant of "One," "Two,"
"Three," "Throw!" out over the
water I fly, the happiest, most
gratified being on earth.

## miss

it hurts, this strange loveless place.
getting there is too much like a motorcycle ride,
its rush of unwanted air
stinging with bugs and flying debris,
a dangerous freedom you
can't wait to wash out of your hair
and leave behind.

others stare, wonder whether they too
might brave a Harley flirt with limb near
disaster, you just want off, want to thank
the leather vested guy you are holding on to
and walk away, your prayer for a stoplight
turning red is your first traffic prayer

but probably not your last since you are
stopped where your angry former love stops
when riding home if the intersection signal
commands **STOP** and you pray that it does
as if what you are asking for makes sense
to God when He knows you could have asked
for a hundred other things that even you know
matter more

and you say just this once as if you had never
said *that* before this particularly painful
heartache,
as if you had not come on to Him before
with your ditzy request that,
since he was extinguishing
so many species, would He please do spiders next
and you wonder what your
praying limit is and whether, if the light changes,
you've used up your last one,
the one you meant to save

for love's *next* mishap,
one you wouldn't want
Him

to miss

B. Koplen

While completing an M.A.T. in English at Converse College (1970), Barry won his first prize for poetry in 1969. His poetry collections include *Broken Homes, Broken Hearts*, and *Father's Day/Mother's Day Canceled*. Another chapbook, *GIRLs STORE*, revolves around women's issues. His poetry has been published in area journals, newspapers, and worldwide on the Net. Early in 1998, Barry was appointed poet laureate of the Purple Heart House and its Wall of Hope in Hollywood, Ca. His poem "Joseph" was published in 2004 in *The Breath of Parted Lips*, Voices from the Robert Frost Place.

B. Koplen

## conniving

old blues crawl and claw like a forgotten dog
tied to a rusted chain; there is a low wail,
a sound as piercing as an unfretted chord
low on the narrow neck of a passed down
six string;

it calls as its flailing notes unlatch
that hidden locket the world is not
supposed to see inside; its pain-bearing words
cull rank emotion with a savvy screech
as pitiless as the tearing sound of a wind twisted
branch
snapped off a living tree;

its dance floor is an open wound, an
unhealed scar, a malnourished passion;
it feeds our unfed parts; it makes
our tears well and tremble as if
they, too, pulse with
bad news and troubled times;

it clings to our drying clothes
hanging on the two string line where worn
shirts and pants advertise our condition
and make known our frailty as if
we are shoddy soldiers, sad warriors
armed only with ragged blues

until B.B. King rolls out
in a limo stretched longer than
a deep-chested menacing howl
aimed at a conniving moon

B. Koplen

## bomb

an ageless string of pre-Ike houses
front Main
like a permanent display.

cars pass slowly in April
for their annual show of
punchy azaleas
innocent of time,
busting with hope-retrieving blooms

that May turns brown
with brute force unmistakable
as a deftly timed
roadside bomb.

## The Muse

The muse keeps prodding;
Not as with cattle prods,
But gently, whispering—
"Take up your pen and write."
No matter that you stumble on the words,
Tripping over each other
Like feet of pidgin-toed children
On a broken sidewalk.
"Put it down in black and white.
Purge yourself.
You will feel emptied
As after a dose of castor oil
Administered by your grandmother."
There may be someone out there
Who will hear you.

## The Mole and the Flower

I am half mole,
Hiding from the world—
—Blind, secretive, digging in the gloom,
Alone in my tunnel,
Hating the light.
But then—
I am half flower;
Opening to the sun,
Adorned in brilliant colors,
Blooming where I'm planted,
Welcoming the bees.

Margaret Peck Latham

(b.1920, Lexington, Missouri)
Graduated from the College of
William and Mary with a degree
in psychology. She earned her
M.aster of Nursing. at what is now
Case Western Reserve School of
Nursing. She lives in Charlottesville,
Virginia. Her work has appeared
in several volumes of *The Poets
Domain*, and she has made five
collections of her poetry.

## Residuary Inventory
*(. . . d'une femme d'un certain age)*

In spite of problems varicose and adipose,
At least, thank goodness, she's not yet comatose. . . .
And senior discount is a *plus* that she can stand
(Even when proffered these days
      *before* demand.)
Though the mambo and the cha-cha-cha
      have been missed,
She's becoming expert at the "pelvic twist."
Morning jogging's out—her jumpsuit's
      gathering lint . . .
Now, at night, she's running the
      brisk bathroom sprint.
A certain jaunty carriage of her head, you say?
The better to see you, my dear! (The *only* way . . .
Through bifocal lens she finds—
      with resigned sigh—
She can see more clearly
      with her head held high!)
After multimileage, the chassis
      shows some wear—
Due to replacement of parts needing repair.
(More careful maintenance might have
      spared wear and tear—
But special parking perks
      are burdens she can bear.)
"Older's better than the other option,"
      she'll concur.
Unhappy being *d'un certain age?* Morose?
      Not her!
In spite of problems varicose and adipose,
At least, *grace a dieu*, she's not yet comatose. . . .

Mary Antil Lederman

(b.1925, Los Angeles, Calif.)
A.B., *magna cum laude*, Syracuse
University, 1946; M.Ed.,
University of Virginia, 1968;
retired in 1987 after 23 years as
foreign language teacher/chair at
Albemarle High School in
Charlottesville, Va. The Senior
Center in Charlottesville now offers
bi-monthly *Cercle Francais* meet-
ings, started by Mary and one of
her former AHS students. Her
poems are in twenty-one volumes
of *The Poet's Domain* and have
appeared in several other national
publications, including the 1993
and 2003 anthologies of the
Poetry Society of Virginia, of
which she is a long-time member.

*Mary Antil Lederman*

## Mirror, Mirror, on the Wall . . .

In this mod, throw-away culture,
On a mad, disposable spree,
I am doing my level best
For more prudent ecology.
With chemically restored tresses,
New metal hips, prosthetic knee,
I admire through plastic contacts
A brand-new recycled, ME!

## My Life

I'm not afraid of death,
I said to myself in a quiet voice,
sitting in an empty room,
staring out the window at some new-fallen snow.
Because God is omnipresent,
even in my empty room fronted by whiteness,
as cars go by as in a dream
and the sky is obscured by clouds.
And even though the wars continue
somewhere in a battlefield of a town
whose name is unpronounceable
but for the language of sorrow.
I could be a leaf but the leaves are gone,
the bare branches are like bow strings
playing the usual sounds of winter,
the wind blowing over a snowy field.
Somewhere there's a melody to unite these
forces—
the cars, the fields, the snow outside,
or better to say it's an unchanging light
as when the sun breaks through the blinds.

Joseph Lewis

(b. 1948, Pittsburgh, Pa.) has
been published in several previous
volumes of *The Poet's Domain*.
He lives in Williamsburg, Va.

## Joy

Joy in the morning with rosy-fingered dawn
in making a cup of coffee in an old white pot
in shaving off two-day growth of beard
in buttoning my shirt like all good citizens
in listening to an old favorite on the radio
in the perfect stillness of a room
        without newspapers
in my new stack of books even though unread
in my new belt, my old shoes, my bad eyeglasses
in some greeting cards with Christmas trees
        I forgot to send
in throwing out the garbage to make my room clean

Joseph Lewis

in the perennial dripping of the morning rain
in the coming spring even though ice is mystical
in finally seeing the stars for the first time
in sweeping the rug, cleaning the commode
and dusting lamps as meditation
in staying up all night completely sober
to ponder the meaning of the cosmos
cosmos, cosmos, everything whirling
in the cosmos
all the poems I've read and every scene
from all the movies
including the ones that were profound
and quite gloomy
not to mention novels like *Don Quixote*
and *I the Jury*
all are a part of the billions of bright
galaxies whirling perfectly
with my memories of childhood and strange
sexual encounters
which would have been better
if we'd been in love
love in the whirling cosmos
with all the poems and sad rooms
where rosy-fingered dawn comes
through the dusty window
to forget somber thoughts and
the television of gloom
joy in the morning as the sun
comes over the trees!

## The Bark of Emptiness

deepening the darkness
        the distance
from the mind of slumber

dogs howling
reaching into ten thousand
years of instinct
waiting in the silence of an unmade bed

## Waiting

D. S. Lliteras

Has a master of fine arts degree.
He is the author of nine books,
which have received national and
international acclaim. In the last
nineteen years, his poetry and short
stories have appeared in numerous
peridocals and anthologies. His
most recent novel, *The Silence of
John*, was published in March
2005. He is a retired professional
firefighter and lives in Virginia
Beach, Va. with his wife, Kathleen.

for all the leaves.
Looking
at Autumn's accumulation.
Walking
upon the fallen leaves and
hearing
the brown brittle sound of their crunching.
Moving
through the light of this season through the
gap of trees changing.
Form becoming emptiness
no . . .
blue changing into green!
the sky replacing
the dense foliage
Blue branches instead of green.
You. Where is the emptiness? in between the
trees? And you. Where did Fall begin? with
the leaves? or, with the sky?
Crunching as I walk.
Listening to their brown brittle sound.
Feeling the warm Autumn sun.
Falling upon forgetfulness.
Rejecting either and or.
Autumn is in the wind.

D. S. Lliteras

## Toward Winter

Through a window
for the first time this season
seeing the wind in the trees
and the coming of winter in the grey sky;
hearing the cold in the rustling of leaves
and the silence behind the clarity
of plate glass.
Through a window, feeling the suddenness of
the other senses and caught for the first time
in between the seasons.

# Echo (of a) Cardiogram

I saw my heart today,
and my mind gamboled in a dozen different
directions.
It wasn't a brilliant red valentine,
with symmetrical shape and smooth curves.
Actually, it seemed rather amorphous.
It doesn't look like a container
that holds a lifetime of love.
When I offer someone 'heartfelt thanks'
I don't think it relates to that critter on the
screen.
When I am speaking 'from the heart'
I am certain it is not from that relentless pump.
Ever notice how often 'heart' and 'soul'
appear in the same sentence or song verse?
I saw my heart today; didn't see my soul.
That blob on the screen was working -
I mean REALLY working hard.
Every second or so - lub dub - lub dub - lub dub.
It's been beating that incessant rhythm
for every minute of every hour of every day
of every month for seventy-two years.
At night, I rest; it never rests.
*Did my parents receive a warranty on my heart?*
"I don't think so."
*Did they sign a maintenance agreement?*
"If so, they never told me."
*Is there such a thing*
*as a limited warranty on one's heart?*
"Yes - it's called term life insurance."
I saw my heart today:
lub dub - lub dub - lub dub.
It was awesome; it was eerie.
My very life depends
on that tireless engine of repetitive action.
I wanted to stand up and cheer for it;
perhaps a prayer would be more appropriate.

*Edward W. Lull*

began his professional career as a
naval officer where he served pri-
marily in submarines. His second
career was as an executive in hi-
tech system design firms. He has a
baccalaureate degree from the U.S.
Naval Academy and a masters
degree from The George
Washington University. Mr. Lull
began writing poetry at age 65. In
1998 he joined The Poetry
Society of Virginia, and served as
its president for four years. He has
published poems in several
anthologies and periodicals, and in
2003, Mr. Lull published his first
book, a historical novel written in
blank verse, entitled *Cabin Boy to
Captain: a Sea Story*.

## Happy as a Hobbit

I am happy as a hobbit
sprawled out on my recliner,
pipe pleasant sweet smoke of
lime and lavender, tantalizing
tobacco with a smile upon my
face.
I pour some brandy and sip,
relishing the years, warm
refinement as orange red and
yellow flames crackle against
wood below my mantle;
my shadow and miniature
pinscher, Rocky, provide the
only needed company.

## One Small Voice

In my head remains one small voice,
always prodding me to make and respect
the best choice.
I remember the words and sounds that
come to me in the dead of night so vividly,
images of an audience too large to count.
The words from a musician or sometimes a
poet from a century or two ago.
One small voice visits me encouraging me
on to fulfill my destiny. My principles
mean more than money and success can buy. . . .
One small voice is the reason why.
Passion and persistence ignite my fire,
my soul energy force is a live wire.
One small voice takes me to the stage,
thousands will watch by the truth of the
final page. The words I write and the
music I play, led by one small voice,
now and forever guides me on my way.
My dreams are reality; listen to your
one small voice today.

*Christopher Hugh Lythgoe*

has been writing poetry since
1999, and is being published for
the second time here. His first
appearance was in volume 21.
The themes of his poetry include
love, war, music, and spirituality.
He is also a drummer who has
played in various bands since
1988 and released a CD entitled
*Cornered with Last Second
Comeback*. Chris lives in Northern
Virginia with his Miniature
Pinscher, Rocky, and works for the
State Department.

## Of Time and Place

Among the half-dead trees, I came upon
the true ease of myself. . . .
—Theodore Roethke, "The Rose"

We are not what we do.
We are not where we live.
The iris grew up blue.
Words are gifts meant to give.
We are where we have been.
We are part of our kin.
Jazz has limited repetitions;
It is more a cactus garden
Not a long stemmed lyrical rose bouquet,
A prickly music surviving drought,
Free to flower in a riff once after
The desert storm in late summer.
We rejoice being home
In a new place, a new time,
Without stones from the Pacific;
No rose in coastal winds climb.
We are at ease among pines,
Purple wisteria blooms strung,
Tangled around half-dead trees hang as beards;
Blossoms fall from limbs. We feel the rough pelts
Of palmetto palms. We sense the sage, see birds
Eat berries in wax myrtle bushes wild
        along the coast.
Our fathers grew no roses in greenhouses—still
We know the cinnamon smooth skins
        of crepe myrtles.
We celebrate our anniversary.
One son sends music in his written words.
One son, his wife Amy, and their three Cs,
Send tulips & blue iris. Spring defers
To lemon yellows. We plant a pair of tiger lilies;
Rejoice in greenhouse cuttings;
        learn to be at ease.

Michael Hugh Lythgoe

(b.Evansville, Ind.) holds an
M.F.A. from Bennington College.
Recent publications include: *Aries,
Windhover, Yemassee, Texas Poetry
Calendar 2005, Christianity and
Literature*, and the anthology,
*Poems of Francis and Clare*, St.
Anthony Messenger Press. He has
appeared in the last 17 volumes of
*The Poet's Domain*. Mike is a
retired Air Force officer, and a for-
mer history teacher. He recently
moved with his wife, Louise, from
Virginia to Aiken, S.C.

Michael Hugh Lythgoe

## To Pay the Boatman

Every river crossing is an obstacle;
Dante's river is darkness too deep to wade.
Frost tells us the way out is the way through.

Rivers, after Dante's cantos, lead to glades
Inside an Inferno, to join suffering ghosts.
In dark woods, one imagines many shades.

My love and I find Kelly's Ford, pay the cost.
Safely we cross the Rappahannock River;
Move through winter fog, avoid getting lost.

To be lost in the dark is to live with fear.
I hum Hoagey Carmichael's tune, *Winter Moon*;
March night is moonless; I feel sixty winters.

Battle grounds: Cedar Mountain, mortal wounds,
Brandy Station, Chancellors Ville, The Wilderness.
Ghost riders are cavalry, gray dragoons.

Hoagey Carmichael's ballads anchor my past,
Transport me to Indiana, where he sings
Still for my dead parents whose love song lasts.

Legendary boatman lifts coins off eyes, brings
Damned souls over the river Acheron;
Charon—haunting, poling, night shrouding.

Finally, the lights, the bridge, the Inn,
Comforting fireplace, musket over mantel,
Birthday drinks, meal before the summons.

Charon leaves me among the living, no bell.
We return a different way, by-pass the boatman
Of the Underworld, the ferry to a literary Hell.

Life is crossing rivers, however wary,
Aging on a moonless night, dangerously
Aware of a little more time to love, not unwary

Michael Hugh Lythgoe

Of what I left upstream: cancer's scare—happily,
News from our children, their children, and death,
An aunt. Downstream—rivers, vulnerability:

Tigris and Euphrates, war. On shore, my breath
Inhales a smokey mist obscuring Hades, river;
I hear poetry and pain; warriors facing death.

Sunrise melts dirty snow to muddy rivers.
Fog burns away. Pray let the ferryman
Row another day or way, other passengers.

The grim reaper is an aging boatman.
Poor souls may cross or stay: I'll try Potomac—
White's Ferry—miss creaking oars of Charon.

## Rosebush Recollection

In my mind's eye, I'm viewing
    a rosebush now in blossom.
It grows in the far corner
    of a small garden triangular shaped,
It sits just in front of an old brick wall.
    There it was planted
By my grandfather with small help from me
    that he'd requested.
My grandfather was the cherished mentor
    of my boyhood days,
And always he requested my help
    on tasks that were ones
Accompanied by how-to-do-it instructions
    meant to ensure
That soon I'd master that task
    and many others on my own.
The planting of the rosebush
    done in partnership with
My grandfather was one
    of the earliest sessions with him
As teacher, but I recall it often
    and easily for it is indelibly
Inscribed in memory and has burrowed
    its way deep into my psyche.
For that rosebush and the flowers it bore,
    I developed a proprietary
Interest. I watched it and nurtured it
    through each growing
Season during my kid years
    in knee pants to the long-pants times
Of adolescence and burgeoning manhood.
In these years when young manhood days
    are long gone,
Even middle age does not fit
    who and what I've become,
For now I'm in my late years
    that are getting later at a pace
That does dismay. But still,
    whenever some triggered memory
Of Grandpa enters my consciousness

*Seymour Z. Mann*

is professor emeritus, CUNY,
where he served on the faculties of
Hunter College, John Jay College
doctoral faculty in Political
Science. His poetic efforts were
included in seven previous volumes
of *The Poet's Domain*, and he is
honored to have his poems in the
company of fellow poets and
friends whose work also appears in
the pages of this volume.

Seymour Z. Mann

it is accompanied by my internalized vision
    of the rosebush by the wall—as the case
Is at this moment; however,
    as the memory of grandfather
As mentor to me was coursing through me,
    like a computer-
Generated photo slide-show, my mind's eye
    vision of the bush
Revealed pictures of it at the various stages
    of its life, and
Projected on the screen now is mother bush
    almost denuded
Save for one tired-looking flower
    barely hanging on with
Most of its now-wrinkled petals
    having fallen to the ground.
The last slide of the show comes into view,
    and what I see is
The last rose's last petal wafted
    by a quiet breeze so it flutters
In the air before it too descends to the earth
    below, summer is
Over, the last rose has died
    and the bush that hosted the flowers
Will soon fall into a state of dormancy
    hoping that spring's
Warmth will make it live again.
    And in my head I'm hearing
What grandfather told me in the first winter
    after we planted the
Bush in front of the old brick wall was:
    *Don't worry grandson, the bush will make it.*
*We'll take care of it, so by midsummer it will dis-*
*play for us the splashes of color to feast our eyes*
*and offer the sweet odors exhaled from the roses to*
*languish in our noses.*
O, what a wonderful and telling recollection
    I've experienced.
The reality of it may have happened
    in my long-gone early
Youth, but the meaningfulness of it
    is what steadies me in
My dwindling years.

## Ribbons, Medals, Not Anything More

Queued according
To family and hue
Waiting for all
The judges to view

When the judging
Of flowers was done
The young child beamed
Her mother's had won

Let's take them home
And put on display
Blooms and ribbons
The young child did say

*John G. Marshall*

(b.1948, St. Mary's County, Md.) is a fishmonger by day and a writer wannabe by night. Much of his poetry is flavored with the experiences of fellow Vietnam Veterans. John and his wife, Vivian, have been happily married for thirty-five years and live in Poquoson, Va., with their cat, Ellie.

Take the ribbons
The mother assured
Ribbons only
Not anything more

The young girl sad
By Mother's response
She remembered
A like circumstance.

Like her Daddy
Who went off to war
Got back medals
Not anything more.

John G. Marshall

## Magnifying the Past

The conflict was over.
They said that didn't they?
Not victors that April of '75—
Survivors.

And those who had gone before
Knew the terrible secret.
The one we who had yet to return
Would soon learn.

Our conflict had just begun.

The reliving of so many months
Of long days and longer nights
Where our stories,
With their intense, intricate detail,
Would all too often raise questions
About tomorrow's weather
Leaving us to stand alone
In the crowd of family and friends
Who had become more like strangers
Who wondered:

Why we couldn't fit in,
Why we would drink too much,
Why we lost our sense of humor,
Why we kept the lights on all night,
Why we couldn't keep a steady job,
Why we kept looking over our shoulders,
Why we would flinch at any sudden sound,
Why we roamed through the house at two a.m.,
Why we kept a round in the chamber of the gun,
                Tucked under our pillow,
Why we would sit for hours with blank stare,
That said, "I'm in a place where you can
never go."
Why we would cry.

John G. Marshall

Whiskey and smokes soften the edges
Of memories better forgotten.
We sit hunched over a table
Bathing in the security of harsh light.
We see the muzzle flashes
From distant tree lines, hear
The zip of passing missiles,
The sickening smack of one finding a target,
The agonizing screams
That wrench our guts
Until we finally realize the screams
Belong to a shell of a man
Sitting at a kitchen table
With half a bottle of amber fluid
And an overflowing ashtray.

He tries
To wash away the images
Of earlier battles,
But for that
There is never enough whiskey;
Only enough to mute the present
And magnify the past.

## No More Ivory Towers

Love and kisses
said the frog
will set me free.
Foolish pride,
ivory tower,
the open window
looking over the town square—
bound up. Shut I the
outside world and
kept myself in a locked chamber.

Love and kisses
said the frog
will set me free.

I listened to the
lure of the outside world.
I chopped my hair today, braided I a ladder,
twined together, my hair, years, and cares and
bound
my fears away, inched down my cold walls.

Love and kisses
said the frog
will set me free.

I will be no more in the tower kept
by witch or prince,
I will listen to the song of the world,
I will no more listen to the songs of frogs,
whisper of witches,
pleas of princes,
my song will set me free.

Megan K. McDonald

started writing in a junior high
school creative writing class in
Hawaii, but other than a yearly
Christmas poem did not write for
twenty years. She has been pub-
lished in *Poet Anonymous'*
anthologies; *Poetry Just for You*, a
local Reston poetry magazine, and
*Event Horizon*, a local Frederick
poetry/art magazine.

Megan K. McDonald

## Taking the Next Step—
## Lake Anne Reflections

Little steps, big steps,
waiting to be born,
surrounded by air,
cocooned by life,
breaking free to face the world.

To satisfy an old childhood dream,
waiting to be surrounded by water,
cocooned by a bubble of air,
taking the first step to delve
the waters to glide through
the pool leading to the blue
ocean world. Stepping stone
to plunging deep inside me.

To satisfy my fantasy,
reality sets in, friends say,
how many writers make their
living through writing
and you're only a poet.
Surrounded by waves of words,
cocooned too long by idle fingers,
taking the step to plunge deep
inside me, pulling lines away,
shedding my skin on paper,
molting, facing the world
A *poet*.

## Perspective

You shine your light upon my back
    and cast my shadow before me.
Are my days but shifting grains of sand
    or as words carved in stone
    and spoken by many mouths?
From generation to generation
    to whom is a stone of no consequence
    or a gem without worth?

## To My Mother: Chicken Soup

*Mary Burton McKenzie*

grew up in Richmond, where her
ancestors lived in pre-Revolutionary
days. She began to write and con-
tribute poems to periodicals in
grade school at Westhampton. In
high school at St. Catherine's she
studied with Margaret McGing.
Currently she lives in Atlanta with
her husband, Kermit, and cats,
Max and Marcus Aurelius.

Dear witch, till all hours you brew
Potions adorable, and you
Chant incantations to the lambent gods
Beseechingly, as though you knew
I falter often, even as I plod
Brightly heavenward, determined.

## Lazarus on the Son

Jesus, I would love you, agape eternal—
    Yet mistily you elude me and I find
Historically, enigmas. Mythically my mind
    Accepts fulfillment of our deepest needs
On timeless levels. Yet an old satanic fear
    That in our want we have projected on the skies
Question and answer, uneasily, waiting lies
    In the raw consciousness. Yearningly we grope
For an earth certainty to bind us all
    Till the age end.
        Is there a star somewhere?
A manger still in Bethlehem, shining and fair?
    And do the angels sing to every shepherd?
Today no other answer can I give
But "See, I once was dead, but now I live!"

Mary Burton McKenzie

## Frames of Reference

I look in my mirror and see
a wrinkled old child
wounded and weak.
You see a goddess
wise and compassionate.
With simple awe
I bless your eyes.

I look at you and clearly see
prophecies fulfilled
magic and power,
where perhaps you view
the frightened boy
who left your heart
long, long ago.

## Song

Why do I feel exalted, Oh Lord,
And why do I sing praises,
To you whom I have hated heartily
For my poor desolation?

Have I at last forgiven you
For anguish you seemed to ignore
And for deaths you did not prevent
Since the world's beginning?

Long I have blamed you, Lord,
For poor human pain, for lost freedom,
No chance to choose, only to fail and suffer.
This was my view, Lord.

Perhaps now I will extend
My broken hands.

## Mystery

Miracles are not all sensational.
Some steal like mist
into a house
filling it with joy:

Mary Burton McKenzie

unfeeling hands touch
with magic,
dim eyes flash
with lightening,
and sleeping rituals
rise to life.

How does love come?
Who knows
what mystery,
what gods conspire,
what galaxies collide
in benediction.
Then angels sing
and shepards gape
in splendid awe
at indescribable creation!

## Waiting at the Vet

Dear old dog,
(accompanied by
red-necked, gum-chewing
cowboy-booted, tight-jeaned
complaining owners
ordering you to lie down
because you scratch
because you itch
because you're sick
and full of fleas
and little hair
shields you lean bones)

Your wise old eyes
say, "Patience.
Life is but a little time:
The cycles of motherhood,
the hum of days,
the good pats, the good food,
the good sleep. . . .
Don't worry about
what people think.
They will know
what our love is."

## Persistence

Pain gives the person
a certain sort of patience.
So does failure,
The sense of the undone,
one following another
or just the rare one.
One can practice endurance
without being Spartan.
There are many ways to dance
And many steps we can advance.

## High School History

With gracious condescension
settling down in state
the Queen regals in her throne
among a rapture of robes
untelevised but with similar aplomb
the Belle of the Classroom
commands all eyes
as she rests her thighs
on the saddled seat behind
the heart-scarred desktop

James McNally

(b.1924, Washington, D.C.) is most proud of his schooling at Washington-Lee High School in Arlington, and Jefferson's university in Charlottesville, Va. He taught college English for thirty-five years, twenty-nine of them at Old Dominion University. With Mary, his wife of fifty-five years, he lives in Norfolk on the banks of the Lafayette that grows murkier each year. His work has appeared in several of The Poetry Society of Virginia anthologies.

Frank N. Megargee

(b.1917, Philadelphia, Pa.) is a
retired newspaperman now free
to write what comes to mind.
This is his eleventh appearance
in *The Poet's Domain*.

## Born Again

After sickness,
walking in the park,
not going anywhere,
just soaking in
the warmth, and light,
thankful to be
in this here and now,
with all this color
sucked from earth
and flung aloft
on every side
to make a spring
I almost missed.

## Surprise

Who is that
rushing by
lugging all those
shopping bags,
flustered, harried,
looks familiar.
Why it's me!
or rather I,
reflected in
that shop window,
as I scurry through
my weekly chores.
What a way
to learn you are
just passing by,
no longer young.

## Against the Green

In my mirror through years of shaves,
I've watched me turn a stranger to me,
my face redrawn by criss-crossed lines,
sagging into a fleshy pouch, all flip-flobby
beneath my chin,

Frank N. Megargee

until I ask, who's this weird guy?
For inside I'm the same young me,
ever surging with zest for life
and shocked by what's going on outside,
yet all the while I can't deny
it's death out there acreeping in,
just as it browns an autumn leaf,
first crisping the outer edges,
then working in against the green.

## Old Age I

God, it's awful to be old,
mornings are the worst of it,
getting creakily underway.
Not finding things exactly where
you disremembered putting them,
glasses, hearing aids, teeth, and cane.
Slowly you take human shape,
trying out new aches and pains,
girding yourself to face the world.
A bit of food, then step outside,
birdsong, flowers bathed in light,
neighbors, passersby, all nods and smiles,
telling you it was worth the try,
this one more chance to say goodbye.

## Old Age II

God, it's great, this being old,
mornings are the best of it,
another day that's all your own.
No boss to please, no kids to feed,
no pressure to be here or there,
no one expects you to perform.
Lingering blissfully in bed,
master of loafing, without guilt,
because it's morning you get up.

A bit of food, then step outside,
birds and flowers crazy with sex,
frenzied neighbors late for work,
anxiety-free you watch them go,
glad you're no longer in the flow.

## Musical Smiles

The eyes start
opening notes of
the smile prelude;
The cheeks enter
mezzoforte, a harmony line;
The mouth joins
as a soloist;
The whole performance
a warm euphonious
major chord;
a cheerful climactic overture
of gums and pearly whites.

*Vic Mickunas*

is a pediatrician and parent in the
tidewater area of Virginia. He
started writing poetry after being
inspired by his son Steven and
other local poets who read or recite
at various venues around the south-
side Hampton Roads area. He draws
ideas from experiences in pediatrics;
Masters swimming, in which he is
a regular participant; his time
growing up in central Florida; and
just about anything else that occa-
sionally pops into his head.

## Father God

Unlike the Tin Man in *The Wizard of Oz*,
You gave me a heart.
More courage than the cowardly lion,
More backbone than the scarecrow,
Dropped from a post in a hay field.
You guided me Lord, as I forged my way,
Out of the inner city, out of the dysfunctional home,
Into the Emerald City,
And the arms of the man,
Who has cared for me for half a century.
Father God.
You led me down the yellow brick road,
Watched from above, as I made my way
Through trials and tribulations,
Stumbling off the righteous path, into poppy fields,
Away from you, Sweet Jesus,
And yet you kept the wicked witch at bay.
Lord, you allowed me to become a mother,
Grandmother to a bunch of little munchkins,
Now grown, and a great grandmother,
All of whom shower me with the love and affection,
Dorothy gave to Aunty Em.
I thank you, Father, for being the tornado in
my life,
Whisking me up like the house where Dorothy
lived,
Keeping me safe from harm, and setting me down
In the Land of Oz.

*Helen Mills*

is a Virginia Beach artist and poet. She has been a member of the Chesapeake Bay Art Association for over 20 years and is a member of the Virginia Beach Writers' group. She is currently enrolled in numerous writers' workshops, and her poetry has been published in *VWC Review*, a local university poetry publication. She recently had a short story published in *Moondance*, an international ezine for women.

## Private Place

There is darkness here but I can see out.
So . . . I am not afraid,
This place is mine and mine alone.
No one may enter . . . save God . . . Who is
here always.
I see Him smiling . . . even in this darkness,
Sometimes I am evil . . . and He smiles.
Most often I am good . . . and He smiles.
All is secret here . . . in my private place.
Always . . . forever . . . and forever.
Its windows are as two-way mirrors
No one can see inside . . . I am safe here
where I exist . . .
One inch . . . behind my eyes.

Kent Mills

(b.1942, Norfolk, Va.) grew up in southern Virginia, the heart of tobacco country. His winters and schooling were in a small city, while all his summers were spent on his uncle's tobacco farm. This dual lifestyle of country boy/city boy has greatly contributed to his writing style. Kent writes mainly for pleasure and hobby and is the author of the book *Once Upon a Time, When Tobacco Was Good*. He describes his poetry style as "Punchline Poetry" and attempts to weave his heritage of southern Virginia humor into all his writings.

## Star of Wonder

What child was this—
who stood
on dark street
staring
at small flower
night-blooming cereus
this summer night shining
alone
in darkness?

*Merrill Miner*

is the pen name of Nancy Merrill
Miner Canning. Born and raised
in Philadelphia, Ms. Miner
received a B.A. from Barnard
College and Columbia University;
and an M.A. from Stanford
University. A former high school
social studies teacher in Williamsburg,
Va., Ms. Miner has also taught
English in Tokyo, Hong Kong,
and Nanjing, China. She currently
teaches Suzuki violin in her home
studio in Williamsburg, Va.

## epiphany

purple night
stars silent
speaking with power
intent, unblinking
sheen of majesty
hallowed ground
aglow in starshine
pine boughs shadowed
silence
holding stillness
telling
message
gift
of grace:
I
am born!

Merrill Miner

## Transparency

Forgive us
for not knowing
ourselves
to ourselves
invisible veiled
in mystery revealed
translucence
bearing
unbearable intensity
essence transparent
why
do we not see
this radiance?

## Gone Again

Softness and warmth smooth away rough
edges as love walks out the door.
Bleakly winter walks in.

Pulling away again . . .
How long?

Confusion's brash and blatant chill numbs.

We've done this ritual so many times,
this knowing love's leaving should become easier.

It never does.

*Lu Motley*

Lu Motley is an adjunct professor
at J. Sargeant Reynolds
Community College where she
teaches English composition. She's
also active with the Arts and
Humanities Program in the
Richmond, Virginia, public schools

## Deep Inside

It all goes deep.
That's what brings you back again and again.
Cause that's what we do—
We irritate and gyrate right inside the brain,
We go to the heart and wake in the deep dark
hours where we leave you thinking how
You hate, cause you can't figure out what it is
we're talkin' bout.
So we take you out and try to make you see
what was there again and again.
And you might not like what you read but you
ride the train.
That's right!
You take the lousy trip and smile.

Lu Motley

# Life Goes On

To stay what I thought was alive . . .

I've died a time or two,
born to what was thought true . . .
it wasn't.

Life, that perilous keeper of time and thought,
ordered anew!
Realization reinvented.

Till all comes flying . . .
knocks us off our feet.
Challenging change.
Destruction . . .
old turned new.

Boldly read rudimentary,
Change again . . . challenge,
Survival dictated.

Deceived,
something new comes,
old friends die.
Ages march.
We survive.

Finally . . . final futility!
Friends gone,
All new . . . strange.

Life's herald sings clearly, "No!
You're needed here for memory if nothing
else."

"Not exactly stimulating,
"But since you insist one more time I will try,"
As I climb back into bed and pull the covers
over my head.

Lu Motley

## For Sara

A bright star kept me from stumbling.
Offered light in dark times.
Offered courage to grow old without fear.
Life given to love . . . lived fully, though
fear pounced,
You led,
looking closely,
Taking apart all the pieces.
Courageous Sara,
I owe you much.

## Stream of Consciousness

I don't remember where.
But we weren't yet married.
You were in a bathtub . . .
I was washing your back . . . praying to get pregnant.

Then we fought and you took that other girl to
the dance.
You sat opposite . . . taunting.
I hated her . . . and you!
I knew you loved me.

Later that year, I sang an aria with the school's
brass band.
When it was over, the audience cheered.
You came on stage, picked me up in your arms,
swung me around, and kissed me right in
front of the whole world!

I used to go to a place to be alone where I'd
pray to forget you.
Instead I missed you more.
Now, you're beyond.
And I can't stop grieving . . .
The thought of you in an urn over at Billups'
Funeral Home,
No one could have put all you were in there!

Lu Motley

You're here, in my thoughts, in my heart, in my
dreams . . . I hate cremation.

Last Thursday, as I drove our youngest to the
train he told me:
"I've got Dad in the back," he smiled wryly . . .
he's so like you . . .
"At least I've got part of him . . . I asked for the
ashes; They gave me some."
"Which part did they give you?" I quipped.
He smiled again as we drove on . . .

When he came back from Antigua, he told me
he had almost left the island and
Forgotten . . ...before he remembered to "dump
the ashes overboard."
So there's a part of you, somewhere in the
Caribbean.

## Old Ones

The old ones used to scare us,
with dirt.

You and me,
more than three they hurt.

Old fashioned taut taunt faces, tracing names in
dust on our tables,
Holding up their gloved fingers . . . "tsk. tsk."
And we?
They knew our response before we cried,
"Oh!
How did that get there?"
And . . .
Like trained white mice we ran after rag to polish.
Allowed them to demolish our trampled esteem
with their—petty, putrid, pathetic rules.
Old fools.

Carped as we swam among sharks inflicted,
who knew well how they infected.

## Today I Will Paint the Front Door Red

as the door of my childhood home
I'll plant pink peonies
in the big back yard
rhubarb by the garage
I will simmer the soup
my mother made
bathe the windows in steam
tonight Lawrence Welk
will play pretty bubbles
while I dance
on my father's shoes

*Maureen Mullin*

is a transplanted Midwesterner
and health educator living in
Virginia Beach, Va. Her work has
been published in the online publi-
cation, *Prairie Poetry*, as well as in
the Chesapeake Bay Poets' anthol-
ogy, *Skipping Stones*.

## Not Here

Sitting in the crow's nest,
wind caressing my face,
blowing my hair gently,
surrounded by the
morning conversation of birds,
and warmed by sun that
fills my empty white cup with light,
I conjure up your smiling faces,
as delighted to be
as the new green leaves
on the live oaks that
make green waves around us.
You once were and were happy here,
your pulses beating out a mute message:
"Life is and it is good."
And so it continues to be
although you are not here
to say so yourselves.

## Talking to Plants

Somewhere I read that plants thrive if you
"talk" to them.
Plants in my home endure under benign
neglect or wither.
I ignore all teachings that would encourage a
green thumb.
My attention labors elsewhere.
Prospect of a long beach vacation made me
consider the African violets.
They would surely die if I didn't take the four
along;
three purple, one white; only two blooming.
On the cottage's screened porch they were as
enchanted as I
by the indirect light and cool, moist sea air.
I made a ritual of blessing them with water
enriched with plant food.

Sarah Munson

Sarah has resided in Virginia since 1974, but was born in Pennsylvania and spent her childhood in North Carolina before living in New York during high school and college. By profession a teacher, she has taught English literature and composition in junior and senior high school, and English as a second language to college students in the Philippines in the Peace Corps, and to elementary students in Northern Virginia.
She has four adult daughters: an environmentalist, a flutist, a lawyer, and a physical therapist. In retirement, her avocations are peace education and poetry.

Sarah Munson

One that had never bloomed pushed out pur-
ple buds that hung like bells.
Another savored shaded light in its green
leaves, but held its own counsel.
I know I smiled and expressed my delight in
the environment we shared.
Now, a month later, summer is carrying away
a pleasurable idleness.
The fourth plant is slowly, slowly growing purple
buds.
A late bloomer, it thanks me for our conversation
by the sea.

### Recipe for a Beach Poem

In a very large bowl, place one sunny day
and a lean strip of barrier island.
Add the generous shade of live oaks
to keep things cool, and the zest of a fawn
frolicking in the sandy backyard.
Top with the summertime phrases of
Carolina wren, Eastern towhee and mockingbird.
Garnish with the rap of builders' hammers
and the red and blue letters sailing behind an
airplane
advertising karaoke at a seaside cafe.

# Cache

Fools.
They say this stuff
is hidden in the house,
in closets,
under beds,
in dresser drawers,
and old notebooks—
Well,
maybe so; but
where there's air
to be breathed,
breathe it;
where there's water
and a thirst,
drink.

Marvel N. Mustard

I am a native-born Virginian. I
attended Mary Washington
College, Tidewater Community
College, Virginia Wesleyan
College, and Old Dominion
University, receiving my masters in
English in 1987. I was born in
Keswick, Va., but have lived in
Tidewater for 50 years.

# I Rejoice in Being What I Am

How long did it take me to rejoice
in being what I am?  For twenty-two
years, I'd been looking, searching
for that elusive being who
I felt was there, but I couldn't
quite get a hold of it—or them.
I tried when my children were in school,
I hid it in dresser drawers, beneath
bras, slips, and pantyhose. When
they were gone, when housework
almost got me down, I'd take it out,
scrutinize it, and put it back, gently.
Now, there is no need for that;
My time is in my hands alone.
I can sit, dream, and write
to my heart's content. I have
found what I looked for:
I Rejoice In Being What I Am.

## Lament of Charmian

In Rome my mistress was mistook
And never a harlot was. Married
            to Caesar, what cared we that he
        had a wife in his foreign
        barbarous land, a ritual we did not know.
Great Isis blessed us here.

Then Caesar died, and Antony came.
My lady was not beautiful,
From an Alexandrine line
            The nose too figured.
            And much too fair. But my papers,
            my curls, made her—
Blackened, braided, lacquered
        Golds, purples . . . ah my craft

—what she was
            fit for Queendom. She ruled, but
so did I. . . . We died together
        by that good omen.
    The work of twenty dynasties to bring her
        to that perfection.
        And together we
Made a story for all time.

*Myreen Moore Nicholson*

Myreen is an English professor
and an art appraiser, as well as a
practicing artist. She has masters
from the University of North
Carolina Chapel Hill and Old
Dominion University. She worked
more than twenty years as a
research librarian, and is complet-
ing a work on the family of Edgar
Allen Poe in Norfolk, Virginia. A
more complete biography may be
found in the Millennium edition of
Marquis' *Who's Who in the World*.
She was an assistant to Pulitzer in
Poetry winner, W. D. Snodgrass.

## Upon Viewing Joan Mannell's
## Stingray Point Lighthouse

My friends, let me sit here, leave me alone
to live again
in the pink blush of dawn at Stingray Point.
Let me watch
the seagulls circle, hear the rhythm
of the sea-green waves
against great gray rocks that guard
this sea castle rising high
in early morning light.

This is Stingray Point Lighthouse far,
far from the sandy beach
where I stood and dreamed someday
of swimming to the ladder
that beckoned just above rocks,
dreamed of standing still and tall
on the lighthouse balcony, tasting
salt in the sea air,
watching white clouds billow.

This is the sea castle that stood sentinel
while I cried
for a sand castle that a sneaky wave
stole from me,
while I laughed when my first love
wrote a letter in the sand,
while we gathered limbs fallen from the pines
to build a fire
that roasted hot dogs and us.

Now decades behind me, I ride again
on the back seat of a skiff,
beside my childhood friend,
out of Jackson's Creek
as the lighthouse keeper, her father,
rows with both oars
across the bay where I never swam
to the sea castle
on gray rocks in the sea.

*Ruby Lee Norris*

is a retired secondary school edu-
cator who specialized in teaching
American literature, journalism,
creative writing, and humanities.
She is a member of the Chesapeake
Writers Club. For more than ten
years she has been garden colum-
nist, photographer, and feature
writer for *Pleasant Living Magazine*.
Her poems have been published in
several earlier issues of *The Poet's
Domain*. She also writes short sto-
ries and local color vignettes about
life on the Middle Peninsula. Her
love for restoring old homes is evi-
dent at Sandy Hook's *Pinegrove*,
her parents' home built by her
great uncle just before the Civil
War. There she maintains a
National Wildlife Habitat.

Ruby Lee Norris

Now we attach pulleys that raise the skiff
beside the balcony.
We store supplies; fill the lighthouse lamp
with oil, light the flame,
curl in our tiny bunks, pretend we're sailors
on a ship.
We wake at first blush to oystermen
in their dead rises
chugging to the channel.

Day by day white clouds scud
across the dawn's russet light
high above the horizon where
sailing ships go by,
where we lower the lighthouse skiff, bait
our hooks, cast our lines
squeal in concert as we hook, land
twenty-seven croakers
slippery silver from the sea.

Another day at dawning great gray clouds
and northeast winds
bring wild dark waves that curl and splash
against the rocks.
At dusk we climb stairs, light the flame
that makes the prisms glow
fall asleep to the roar of wind,
the clatter of raindrops,
while our light burns beacon bright.

Thank you, my friends for leaving me alone
to go again
in the pink blush of dawn
to Stingray Point Lighthouse.

## Belonging

Like gravity
I am with stars
breathing in,
breathing out
making leaves tremble
oceans move.

Like granite peaks
I am with nameless moons
and sea anemones
tucked in rock folds,
my steps press
patterns in sand
send messages to crabs.

When I cry, wind
fills my lungs
with songs of love
and I am space.

## The Ripening

I was in my gold skin
you in your tan,
and we danced
over housetops
across parking lots
dangled our feet from
neon signs while raindrops fell
into our mouths
like fake jewels
from Second Avenue
and everywhere you filled me
with miracle.

Like a new
Artemis,
we chased winds
to fields beyond Hoboken
that greened beneath our feet
and we harvested
each other.

*Virginia O'Keefe*

Virginia is the author of *Speaking to Think/Thinking to Speak: The Importance of Talk in the Learning Process* and *Developing Critical Thinking: The Speaking/Listening Connection.* She is a regional vice president of the Poetry Society of Virginia and has won state and national poetry awards. Her poetry has been published in *Wee Ones, Visions, Virginia Adversaria,* and *The Powhatan Review.* As a freelance writer, she writes poetry for the Harcourt Brace Educational Division and is a poetry consultant for public school teachers.

Virginia O'Keefe

## Yupik Storyknife

My father carved this storyknife
For me when I was just a girl.
See how the curved ivory fits my hand,
Guides my thoughts, gives stories to tell
You, daughter of my daughter,
Who wears her labrets in a woman's way.
Watch my knife draw shapes in the mud,
Two more lines and brother whale appears.
When he speaks my knife listens,
    I will not be caught unless women
    keep silent and obey the men.
My storyknife moves on,
Finds sea lion sunning on a rock.
Hears his warning words to women,
    When you bleed, stay apart.
    If you breathe on men, animals
    hide from hunters.
Elders in the past walked here,
Knew the truths, lived the stories
My knife tells,
    I am like a braided river
    carrying water from glaciers
    across great beds of sand and gravel
    to the sea. My lines merge, diverge,
    always bringing life to earth.

## Safe At Home

Lost and untethered, I question
peripatetic, I turn
Inside lies a hidden reception
where peaceful acceptance is firm
I return to my soul for safety
I land after fighting and pain
And I in humanity's haste see,
it's there that mere mystics remain
I return to the home that made me
the home of my soul is safe
Directed by good for the ages,
it's there I'll remember love's face

Judith Reifsteck, M.D.

is a doctor and writer who lives in
Harrisonburg, Virginia.

## A Pair of Old Loves

Already the sun is on the water,
half-heartedly, in this rainy spring.
Three pelicans are there too, fishing
closer to shore than the crabbers come.
The smell of honeysuckle from untamed
property nearby wafts
throughout the house. And the mocking bird
alarm clocks are going bananas. About
this time former colleagues—full
of vigor or full of woe—are trudging
off to their offices in the far-
away city.

Waking up, or, worse, waking
up to duty, is mercifully
slower these days. The first cup of coffee
Is the best cup of coffee, but also a lonely
one, because it calls to mind
its 'thick-as-thieves' companion—that first
morning cigarette, long since banished
from these premises. Always remembered
nonetheless.

I slide into
the early rhythms of a day
full of promise, like a potter with clay
on his wheel and hands on the clay, or like
a waiting page upon which muses
may scribble. I might grow conscious of
the infernal "to-do" list starting to breathe
down my neck, and get drawn outdoors,
into the fresh air of planting trees,
building decks, even going for groceries.
Or I might withdraw into some inner
space to start a new poem, riding
it out like a stallion or a steer,
until the spirit goes somewhere, or
gets wasted.

*Robert A. Rickard*

lives and writes on Capitol Hill, in Washington, D.C., and at *Laetare*, on the Northern Neck of Virginia. Last year his work appeared in the Poetry Society of Virginia's 80th Anniversary Anthology of Poems. This is the sixth appearance of his poetry in *The Poet's Domain*.

Robert A. Rickard

An outer history and
an inner one—these ineluctable
worlds of action and reflection
compete for attention most days. And this
person of gathering years, indulged
and beholden, still says "yes" to two minds,
as if balanced on a pair of circus horses, or
juggling a pair of old loves.

## Beneath

Below our surface of behavior and expression
energy boils, imaginative and passionate.
Streaming throughout semi-transparent lives—
the subconscious, the soul, and the Spirit—
vie.
Undercurrents of character,
depths unfathomed by others,
areas largely unknown even to ourselves.
Active miracles of the Almighty—
reason to rejoice.

*Dawn J. Riddle*

was born in 1967 and raised with
her identical twin in Portsmouth,
Virginia. She earned her under-
graduate and graduate degrees in
sociology at Virginia colleges:
Mary Washington and William
and Mary, respectively. Ms. Riddle
currently manages the *Mansion on
Main* bed-and-breakfast in
Smithfield, Virginia; and enjoys
hosting the Isle of Wight Writers'
Group there. This is her third
appearance in *The Poet's Domain*.

# Widowed

The endless nights hang heavy
Like a rug across my face,
So dense I can barely breathe.
My hands explore the cold sheets,
Nails claw the mattress, knowing
My husband's no longer here.
He was not just anyone.
He was my special someone.
He loved me for forty years,
We had planned for many more.
Now he cannot warm my soul
Or gather me in his arms.
Cannot ever dry the tears
That flow like endless rivers
Flooding onto my pillow
Thoroughly soaking my bed.
No more say I'm beautiful.
He filled past voids in my life
And now they have reappeared
Like an infinite abyss.
His name echoes in my mind.

Marcia J. Roessler

(b.1939, Indianapolis, Ind.)inter-
nationally published, award-win-
ning, multi-faceted author who
earned a listing as Poet and
Fiction Writer in the *Poets and
Writers Directory*. Marcia has
been published in the Georgia
Poetry Society's *Reach of Song*,
Kells Media Group's *Traveled
Paths*, Enright House of Ireland's
*In The West of Ireland*, Rainbow
Books' *Flyin' High*, and numerous
other publications over twenty years.
Her copyrighted song lyrics in *Bonfire*
and *Walk with Me*, have received
worldwide airplay.

Marcia J. Roessler

## Momma the Survivor

My Momma—endurance runner—
Sinewy warrior and tall
Vowed steadfast to finish each race,
She held fast no matter the odds.

She traveled many intrepid paths
Some arduous but others grand
When negatives piled against her
She drew on spunk and held her ground.

Momma fought valiantly and though
Faced with operations and pain
Survived for more than fifty years
Vowed cancer wouldn't make a change.

Determined she lived by her rules
Until through twilight hours converged
Goliath in his dark dank cape
On horseback came thundering down.

We could sense those menacing hooves
That horseman was fast gaining ground
I tried to shield her in my arms
All the while drenching her with tears

And her last words I'll not forget.
"Most races I've won, no regrets.
Before your father died he said,
He'll be waiting to take my hand."

# Cwm

Lying on the beach watching August breakers
    crest white and
crash as successive avalanches roaring to shore,
the chill of primordial snow drifts against my
    skin. I shiver

boxed in by Ice Age rock and Stone Age ice.
A tumult overwhelms aeons of trackless
    snow and
thunders through the mouth of this upland
    valley I couch in.
Spume sparkles unseen in sunlight and subsides
    awaiting later ages.
Echoes, unsettling to older snow, roll by
    unheard.

Jettisoned here—but not here—I measure the
    barren majesty of this valley.
Yet no bird circles these glaciated slopes
    in chromatic color or song.
No tree has yet grown to gain and lose
    to gain again a season's leaves,
no animal here has seen the need to want
    to walk erect,
and that packing, pairing, protecting will be
    the longest and last to come.

Outside necessity and inside need fix this
    as the time, in the heat of a post meridian sun,
    to dig out from this drift
to risk passage through ice caves known only
    for the growl of howling winds and
to sidestep the unfossiled saber-toothed tiger
which stalks still snowbound ice caves of
    upland valleys and
leaves prints in the sand even here on the August
    beach at Chincoteague.
It's time to melt that ice tiger's rage with the
    flame of inner radiance,
time for this man to come of his age and to walk
    warm sand upright
to take the risk of outstretched arms and palms
    piled with sun.

*Tom Russell*

is a retired administrative librarian and a graduate of Kenyon College and of the University of Michigan. He studied with J.C. Ransom, John Ciardi, William Packard, and Ann Darr. His work appears in volumes 8, 11–14, 16, 20, and 21 of *The Poet's Domain*. Published in a number of other magazines and anthologies, he has given readings in seven states. A former officer of the Poetry Society of Virginia, he resides in Harrisonburg, Va.

Tom Russell

## Beyond the Urals

January essential, the woods are winter stark
in this dazzling 13 degree, star-salted Accomack
    County blackness.
Cold flows as fog flows where the creek
    cuts through the soy bean field.
It seeps into the cabin lying low under
    the table and between the bunks.

Scorched by the flame of mortality
prizing my just being
I write all night
triple layered above and below the belt.
Zhivago, Chopin's nocturnes
    come to mind. . . .

    Dammit! Tonight I am Dr. Zhivago
        hiding out at a summer place in winter.
    Few in frozen boiling Moscow know I'm here,
        and those who know don't *know*.

My exiled wife and daughter are safely in
    Paris. Laura and I may already have met.
    It's that unsigned commitment to our
        binding social contract
that pursues me on horseback through the
        white birch forest beyond the Urals
        and into this glittering Siberia.

    Conscription is inevitable day after tomorrow.

    But tonight I'm really free to do as I must.

## Age-Marks (Villanelle)

A woman's battle scars are not to hide!
Have liposuction, face lift, tummy tuck?
Age-marks say, "Womanhood at her floodtide."

The scars of *Jaws*-men proved them *bona fide*.
By how much more do scars show women's pluck!
A woman's battle scars are not to hide!

These *bona fides* make her dignified.
She's won her way with more than just good luck.
Age-marks say, "Womanhood at her floodtide."

No signs of age? World looks at her cockeyed.
But he who looks and mocks is truly smuck!
A woman's battle scars are not to hide!

In ironing face wrinkles I've no pride.
As soon request some fairy dust from Puck!
Age-marks say, "Womanhood at her floodtide."

There must be scars when she's and he's collide.
Then let the world at yours be wonder-struck!
A woman's battle scars are not to hide!
Age-marks say, "Womanhood at her floodtide."

Lynn Veach Sadler

a native North Carolinian and former college president, is published widely. Her full-length poetry volume, *Like a Dragon's Mouth*, is forthcoming from RockWay Press.

## The Beach Run

I ran beside the surging tide
My face to face with ocean wind.
I strained with each arching stride
To push away the world again.

I ran to what I did not know,
Without regard to time or space,
And left behind the ebb and flow
Of endless thoughts I could not face.

The cadence strummed within my mind
The rhythm of my steps on earth.
The footprints that I left behind
Soon washed away beneath the surf.

I left no signs beside the sea
No markers of my throbbing core
And none who followed after me
Would know the one who passed before.

But when I ran upon that beach
Alone, unbent, head high, heart free,
I had awhile within my reach
A taste of immortality.

Martha S. Scanlon

(b.1942, Tennessee) attended
Duke University and the University
of Wisconsin. She settled in the
Washington, D.C. area to pursue
her career in economic policy
research until retirement in 2002
when she began to explore her love
of poetry through writing.

## Focus

Thoughts, like fireworks on the fourth of July,
Flash across my mind too fast.
I want to grasp them one at a time
And let their bursting colors fill my mind
With magnificent works of art.
But each new flash blocks out the last
Concealing it from my soul
Before I can spin it into gold.
They do not last, these tumbling thoughts,
They do me no good at all.
Instead I tremble in their wake, and dread
When the last spark has died,
And I have left no memory.

## Becoming a Teacher

She stood beside the high, unyielding wall,
seeing only the sky above its solid stone,
and a few lush green leaves lifting to the breeze.
The myriad vibrant sounds and chirps and trills
made her child-heart yearn to reach the other side,
to touch the substance of the shadow glimpsed,
to see what creatures threw those lilting notes
over the wall to dance and play around her.
Even on tiptoe, she could not touch the top.
Was there no way of reaching that unknown?

Farther along, another child, and another
stood still for a moment, wondering and puzzled.
One frowned, than shrugged and quickly turned away
to find a more inviting place to play.
The other, with tilted head and wistful eyes,
crouched suddenly in tearless, mute despair.
Then she saw at the top the busy gardener.
His eyes smiled down at her, but he hesitated,
as though he wished to finish, first, his work.
"I cannot leave this task, my child," he said,
"but follow the marked path around the wall
to the gate." And with a quick, impatient nod,
he turned his back and left her on her own.
Yet, even in her joy of being asked
to join him there, she paused. The gate seemed far,
and, if the inner garden were so fair,
why had the high stone wall been structured there?

She left the crouching, watching, silent child,
the wild, free shouts of garden-shunning boys,
and made her slow, laborious, searching way
to find the hidden lures behind the wall,
cradling in memory the hopeless eyes,
the shrug with which a child had turned away
to easier, more reachable pursuits.

*Shirley Nesbit Sellers*

is a retired teacher of Norfolk schools, resides in Norfolk, and is active in storytelling and in story and poetry workshops. She has won numerous awards in the Poetry Society of Virginia and the Irene Leach Memorial Contests; was second place winner in the National Federation of State Poetry Societies Poetry Manuscript contest (1977) and has published a chapbook, *Where the Gulls Nest: Norfolk Poems*, Ink Drop Press. She is currently serving as president of The Poetry Society of Virginia.

*Shirley Nesbit Sellers*

She wished her pitying arms could rock each one,
and whispered a promise to herself and them.

The years have passed, the gardener retired.
She tends the garden now. The wall is gone.
The garden paths are free to questing feet.
No formal tending ever brought about
a lovelier profusion than is here.
No crouching figures wait. There is no gate—
only the teacher and the waiting garden
lying open to the sun—a world of wonders
to touch and see and hear. To little ones
who reach the crest of the hill year after year,
it suddenly appears, is simply there.

## Femininity Cannot Be Lawed

Femininity cannot be lawed,
Nor womanliness voted out of fact.
I would remain a woman, flesh and mind,
Were I to wield a hammer, wrench, or hoe.
The skies would smile and breeze the plane no less
Were I to man the levers and controls;
Yet life could reach a height as deeply felt
As exaltation sweeping a proud father
When he sits down to rock his new-formed child.
I could see myself, still soft with wonder,
Using a welder's torch, or hauling nets;
Or, with a love for all live things, life-risking
To save a burning home and those within.

But I could never see myself in arms,
Tigress tense, prepared to take my toll.
Never!
    Recalling emptied mother arms,
Long centuries and countless banners old,
In empathy I would refuse to go.

## Summer Afternoon

I keep my floor to myself
4 x 5 space is all I know, all I want
it's where I'm at ease
at peace
it's where I'm clouded and clear
wanted and dear
supplies all nearby, cleverly disguised
useful items, heavily on rotation
after awhile
all scented the same

## Shiver

*Sara Marie Shaw*

(b.1989, Fairfax, Va.) has lived in
Nokesville, Va. all her life. She is
a big fan of writing, whether it be
poetry, stories, or essays. These
poems are her first publication.
She plays the viola, guitar, and
bass guitar and enjoys listening
and playing just about every style.
She also loves photography and
practicing all other art forms. She
aspires to earn a degree in psychol-
ogy while continuing to keep music
and writing always in her life.

cold
cold and sick of being cold
in the tips of my fingers
tips of my toes
it lingers:
envelopes me
sets me back
until I become a simple, primitive motion

## I Never Noticed

by sharing such a random necessity
it's almost like we've kissed
but isn't that our deepest desire,
our hidden little wish?
something to dream about
scream about
scheme about in the early morning hours
oh so lonely and unloved?
they all happen to be the same
all carbon copies after me
each one less potent than the last
they're all just saccharine-sweet.
the unspoken bond is now exposed
oh whatever shall I do?

## The Wildest Wave Alive[1]

O the wildest wave alive!
Human, swimming sea-surging crystal aquamarine,
Off the Italian coast,
Body-surfing through glittering,
Sparkle-irradiated undersurface;
Submerging, emerging, submerging. . . .
Sky—water—wave—diving—
Dolphin leaping, becoming fish,
Streaming green weed, buoyant rainbow bubble,
Supple-sleek seal, magical merperson:
All is brilliance, shining.
One . . . with curl-cresting white foam,
Sun-dazzle, wind-spume,
The great radiant universe,
Light shattering into light,
Into transforming transcendent exultation!
Soaring beatitude:
Browning's *"wild joys of living,"*[2]
In a world momentarily—briefly—forever,
Suspended in rapture, in ecstasy.

*Peggy Shirley*

Due to home schooling by her mother while living in the Philippines, Peggy has had a life-long love of poetry. She has served as a public and an army librarian. This is her third appearance in *The Poet's Domain*. She lives in Williamsburg, Va., with her retired U.S. Army Lt. Colonel husband.

1. *The Rose,*—T. Roethke
2. *Saul,*—Robert Browning

# A Friend from Youth

sent me a note
on a poem, *To The Future*.

Said it reminded him of me,
of things we had in common

when we roomed together as
ministerial students.

I remember
he was a minister's son,

I, a laborer's son,
how both scraped by.

I remember his love of art,
his skill at sketching,

my love of sports, I
wasn't writing then.

I don't remember much
we did together:

that all night stint
on the yearbook,

the weekend we hitched to a
fishing spot, slept

in a corn field
and on a rocky shore,

caught no fish. I
don't remember

we did much else together,
only we were friends.

It was kind of him to
send me the poem.

I think he's still trying
to save me.

*Jerry Smith*

began a career as a language arts
teacher in junior high school on
Long Island, New York. He then
accepted a position with the U.S.
Office of Education in Washington,
D.C. Later, as a professor, he taught
education courses at Syracuse
University and Indiana University.
Jerry has been writing poetry for
eight years. His poems have won
awards in several national competi-
tions and have appeared in antholo-
gies and poetry magazines. He has
read his poems in a variety of set-
tings and has taught poetry lessons
for high school classes.

## The Backyard

Warmth permeates,
Gentle caress of angel whispers,
Youthful glow of springtime,
Chattering of birdsong,
A cool revival,
A soft remembrance,
Life anew.
My world still changes.
Familiarity still awakens.
I feel this.
I feel me.

*Shannon Dorsey Sorensen*

(b.1974, Williamsburg, Va.) stud-
ied at Christopher Newport
University where her work was
published in the literary journal,
*The Beacon.* She was awarded her
associate degree in political science
from Broward Community College
in Ft. Lauderdale, Fla. She is
honored to be published for
the second time in *The Poet's
Domain*, along with her mom,
Sharon Dorsey.

## Surpassing Rainbows

It is not the end of the rainbow that is important.
It is not the pot of gold we seek.
Truth is found in the journey,
Through the misty rays of God's smile.

# Christmas 1930

"It will be different
this year," said Mother
underscoring her warning
with references to Father's
reduced employment schedule,
Uncle Charles's losses
in the stock market,
and other factors too abstract
for me to understand
at the age of nine.

"We are not alone,"
she assured my siblings
and me, referring once again
to widespread unemployment,
desperate people jumping
to their death out of windows
in city skyscrapers
across the nation.  But now
she came closer home
telling us about total
unemployment for two
of her brothers-in-law,
each with a family
on the verge of starvation.

From here she segued into
a request that we
search through clothes, toys,
books, and other possessions
we might sacrifice
to give our cousins a Merry Christmas.

"Nothing worn out," she warned.
"Nothing you're tired of reading,
or wearing, or playing with."

*Bruce Souders*

(b.1920 in Richland, Pa.) has
been exposed to poetry as long as
he can remember: hymns, folk
songs in "Pennsylvania Dutch"
and German, materials in elocu-
tion, poems in newspapers and
children's magazines. A retired
United Methodist minister and
professor emeritus at Shenandoah
University, Winchester, Va., he is
a past president of The Poetry
Society of Virginia and the
Shenandoah Valley Writers'
Guild. He has studied privately
with Judson Jerome, Madeline
Mason, and Chad Walsh. He has
appeared in *The Poet's Domain*
since volume 3.

Bruce Souders

Seeing our quizzical look
she added, "Don't worry.
You'll have your Christmas, too."

Christmas morning came. During
the night, Santa had put up the
tree as usual and put out
presents, such as they were.

My heart fell when I saw my
old express wagon
repainted—not the bike
I had ordered from Santa
at the Bon Ton toy department.

Now, Santa was dead to me
until we delivered our hand-me-downs
to Aunts Florence and Frances
and saw the joy in our cousins' eyes.

That night, something else happened.
I forgave Uncle Charles
for failing to give me a present. Deep
in my heart I thanked him
for giving me the chance to walk
down the aisle of the church in my tattered
bathrobe and homemade crown singing
*We Three Kings of Orient Are.*
Our trio never sounded better.

## A Realist's Manifesto

Because I did not ask to be born,
I, like every living creature,
must make the most of what I am
and what I have. There is no turning
back into the womb again.

Bruce Souders

## After an Evening at the Art Museum

I awoke mid-sleep
to see the full moon peeking
in my window after
its release from banks
of clouds. It reshaped
my room according to
the style of Edward Hopper.

A slant of light rolled
across the floor, a magic
carpet inviting me
to leave aloneness, my joy
in times of stress; but I
refuse the invitation,
afraid to be drawn into Hopper's
spotlighted isolation
where aloneness appears
as loneliness to others—
I cherish my self-esteem.

## Art and Artifice

At times I prefer
virgin sounds of nature
filtered through space, fields,
and foliage in trees and bushes—
    breezes,
    bird calls,
    running streams,
    and waterfalls—
to well-turned melodies.

At other times, I long
to see fluid shapes
and colors in the spotlight
of each season and day—
    snowdrifts by ice set,
    spring flows and springlets,
    sunrise and sunset—
to calculated paintings.

## Counterpoise

A goodly part of me is night,
darkness, oceans swallowing land,
but some of me is morning light
and lilies and roses in my hand.

A lot of me is pain and ache
and dismal day and time of sorrow,
but some of me forgoes heartbreak
and looks with rapture toward tomorrow.

A great deal of me mourns the sun,
no sooner risen than gone down,
yet humerous fabric's soon upon
me like a coronation gown,

arraying princess turned to queen
because of whose crowning there are poured
libations that for years have been
shared by both peasant and highborn lord.

*Margaret Stavely*

(b.1918, Easton, Md.) submitted
her work to several poetry contests
this year, despite health problems
following three surgeries and viral
pneumonia between January 2003,
and January 2004. Although her
output of poetry has slowed, she
revised previously written sonnets
and wrote several new poems dur-
ing March and April. Spring
births of three infants to families of
her great grandchildren increased
the number of Margaret Stavely's
great-great-grandchildren to six.
Since 1996 her poetry has
appeared in each volume of *The
Poet's Domain* series.

# Awakening

In the space between our heads
A cat lies sleeping
Our weekend nap
Luxurious beyond all budgets.

Waking to her purr of total relaxation
I still my breath
Rest myself in trust, dear closeness
And irresistible softness.

Mary Talley

(b.1934, Waco, Texas) is pleased
to have her poetry published in *The
Poet's Domain* for the first time.
Other poems of hers have
appeared in *Icarus* chapbooks, *The
Dead Mule*, and *Skipping Stones*.
Currently, she and her partner live
in a retirement community in
Virginia Beach with two fine cats
and lots of other seniors.

## Strands of DNA

Old pictures, brown, faded, deep mystery
Faces of people long dead stare at me.
Ancestors, their lives preserved by my mother
Her stories of family, esteemed as no other
With great pride she told me of heroes so bold
Brave women and men, a moral stronghold
A child was encouraged by this history
A beacon, a challenge, a message for me
To uphold the tradition, boldly face life
No trembling, no failure, no running from strife.
Now older and curious, searching for detail
Found a serious flaw in my mother's portrayal
Her narrative omitted a slice of real life
The German grandfather who mistreated
his wife
Then were there others, faint-hearted or weak?
Of a few of my kinfolk she did not speak
And I think what I know of biology
The genes, chromosomes bequeathed to me
A swirling cauldron of diverse DNA
Who am I really? I cannot say.

## Dreams

My friend dreams of buying a motorcycle.
She wants to speed down a mountain road,
feel the wind in her face,
an adrenaline rush.
My dream is a surfboard.
I'll start with the small size.
My grandson will teach me
to skim with grace across the waves,
sliding, gliding to a sandy shore.
A purple bathing suit, that's all, no shoes.
I'll wait til the wind blows from the southeast,
then take my board, swim into the swells
and look for that perfect wave.
Spectacular!

*Margaret L. Thomas*

is a registered nurse, a graduate of Ohio State University, and has traveled extensively as the wife of a career military man. She discovered the joy of creative writing at the Lifelong Learning Society of Christopher Newport University. Her work has been published in *The Beacon*, the *Virginia Gazette*, *Beginnings*, and the *Clann MacKenna Journal*. When not writing, Margartet is gardening, reading, knitting, doing volunteer work, or preparing Sunday suppers for her grandchildren.

Robert C. Trexler

(b.1926, Newark, N.J.) is a
retired electrical engineer. He
studied music composition and has
written many songs for which he
also wrote lyrics. His first published
poem appeared in 1946 in a U.S.
Army Air Corps newsletter in
Germany. *Wandering* is the first
poem to be published in *The
Poet's Domain*. Robert lives in
Annandale, Va.

## Wandering

There I go,
Wandering.
Looking for one who will give me love,
Make me whole.

She would be . . .
I don't know . . .
Beautiful.
Fresh as the newborn day.

She would . . .
Be my life,
As my wife,
That is what I say!

Gone again,
Wandering.
Looking for someone who'll
Give her heart to be mine alone.

Need to quit,
Got to quit
Wandering.
I need to find a home.
Home, with a girl who will be my own,
I'll stay at home.
No more to roam.

## The Ballet of Windows

The ballet of windows
Is a dance of seasons,
Frost's breath,
A tracery of star-ferns
Rain weeping down the glass,
And sleet, a rattling flamenco.
The panes catch a dazzle of white,
Swirled from apple blossoms.
Or storm clouds menacing the day.
There is blazed gold,
As the sun's fingers
Graze the evening sky,
A spill of light
Where dusk pulls darkness in,
And leaf shadows snared on sills.

Then, stealthily, secretly—snow,
A final coverlet for sleep.

*Constance N. Tupper*

(b.1919, New York, N.Y.) is a
visual artist who has lived in
Charlottesville, Virginia, for more
than forty years. A member of The
Poetry Society of Virginia, she has
had poems published in volumes
2–19 of *The Poet's Domain* and in
*Orphic Lute*. In 1976 she won a
Merit Award from *Woman's Day*
magazine for her essay, "Women,
Today and Tomorrow." In 1993 she
won a first and third prize in The
Poetry Society of Virginia's annual
contest. She also won an Honorable
Mention in The Poetry Society of
Virginia's 1999 annual contest.

# How I Became What I Am and Will Be

Who am I? Who was I?
I am a bubbling boiling ever-changing
But ever-constant stream
Of who I was, am, and will be.

How did I get to be what I was
And what I am?
How will I get to be
What I could become?
I dreamed of some answers in the night.

My mother taught me to love
to serve
to love learning. My father
taught me to work hard
to love the woods and open sky
to put tools to wood. God
gave me the love of beauty
some ability to create it
a striving after the Good. Public service and
retirement gave me creative platforms to be who
I was and could be.

But the devil gave me messiness
forgetfulness
the need for applause. My wife seeks
to help me overcome these devilish traits—
with very modest success.

I alone am responsible
For doing something with good gifts.
For failing to overcome the devil's gifts.

But then who am I becoming?
Perhaps I will learn in my day dreams or in the night
Or from the still voice of God
(who perhaps has not spoken to me yet).
For now, I seek to learn and to help those who
need help
And care for those who care for me
And some who don't.
Perhaps you can tell me what I should become.

Jack Underhill

has a B.A. from the University of
California at Berkeley, a masters
from Columbia University and
Harvard's School of Government,
and a Ph.D. from George Mason
University; is retired after 42 years
of Federal service; has written a
number of books on new towns; for
seven years has been enrolled in
the poetry workshop of George
Mason's Learning in Retirement
Institute; aspires also to wood
sculpture and painting; is a prac-
ticing grandfather to six grandchil-
dren; has three adult children and
a wife of 44 short years.

## Lost Boy

At three, runny nosed and crying loudly,
I was taken by chalk-white people
to a mission school.
My brothers and sisters and the parents who
adopted me are not part of me.
Neither white nor Indian, where do I belong?
The healing ceremonies and customs of my tribe
are foreign to me.

I look into the mirror and see
high aquiline cheeks sharply edged,
dark eyes, and a face the color of earth.
The face of a young Navajo man.

I've wandered through my life's journey,
in confusion.
When I look at jagged red bluffs and cerulean
skies I think,
Is Mother Earth mine? Is she
closer to the white man's God?
Where are the spirits of my ancestors?

My white parents say I belong to the Navajos.
On a yellow bright fall day,
I return to Monument Valley,
the home of my Navajo family.

The cousins, sister, and Aunt Hodezbah
enclose me in their arms.
They cry, in Navajo, "He has returned home,
he has grown into a man."
Heavy silver and turquoise bracelets
brush my forehead,
my Aunt Hodezbah
with tears running down her cheeks says,
"He has been away, far from us.
We who will love him,
will teach him, and keep him here!"

*Elizabeth Urquhart*

studied English literature and history at the University of Iowa; later earned a master's degree at Old Dominion University, Va. For eighteen years, she was a reading specialist in the Hampton City, Va., schools. She writes poetry, and is interested in gardens, music, and wildlife. Her three children grown and scattered, she lives with her computer scientist husband and four cats. She is a member of the Williamsburg Poetry Guild and The Poetry Society of Virginia. Her poetry has appeared in five volumes of *The Poet's Domain*.

Elizabeth Urquhart

## Gerald Stern—Poet

Bandy legged, dome headed, Gerry,
smiling eyes pierced
those listening, dead quiet, souls
in a sardine packed room,
full of all shapes and sizes.
Sitting on chairs and floor,
quiet and hushed, with
sometimes uproarious laughter,
but riveted to his words!
*Dead dog and walnuts,*
*a chicken with three hearts,*
*lift the murderous hook to free the little mouse.*
A quick to laugh, happy man transforms
the small and insignificant
into soaring, heart-touched poetry.

## Molly Whitegoat's Christmas

Wispy pinon smoke spirals upward,
from a hole in Molly Whitegoat's hogan.
Smoke lost in a sky bright with stars.
Smoke from a rusted out, dangerous, old stove.
A beehive-shaped hogan made of logs,
plastered with mud is Molly's home.
She's stooped and moves slowly.
Her black hair, newly washed in yucca suds
is streaked with grey, and tied back with strips
of red wool.
She wears a worn, green velveteen blouse,
an ancient squash blossom necklace,
full skirt, and heavy boots from the Gallup
A&N.

Elizabeth Urquhart

Her fingers are lumpy and misshapen,
but they still weave on her loom,
rugs to make you catch your breath,
black on red, gray and white,
tan with yei figures,
always with a hole in one corner,
to let the spider woman out.
*It's Christmas Eve,*
*A pickup truck parks on the canyon floor,*
*Two men from St. Michaels's mission come*
*lumbering up the hill*
*carrying a stove, for Molly,*
*for Molly Whitegoat's Christmas.*
*They gather round the stove,*
*there's laughter and hot coffee.*
*There's warmth and comfort in Molly*
*Whitegoat's hogan on Christmas Eve.*

## Adventure

My bare feet climb the prickly rope ladder,
backpack clinging to my shoulders,
heart beating fast.
Pinpricks of perspiration dot my forehead.
I reach between the rope strands
and touch rough, mottled, brown sandstone.
Don't look down!
The canyon floor, covered with scented silver,
sage brush, lies far below.

I crawl over the top. In front,
are crumbling dusty Anasazi cliff dwellings,
which shelter secrets of the past.
A deep pit, a kiva, with faintly painted walls,
was a sacred place where elders ruled
and discussed the laws of the tribe.

Elizabeth Urquhart

I find a small translucent skull,
surrounded by turkey bones,
gray and black pottery shards
and bits of corn. The skull,
perhaps exposed by desert scavengers,
rests in my hands:
I see a laughing, bronze skinned child,
dressed in soft skins and plaited yucca sandals,
running from her parents on the canyon floor.
My descent is perilous,
feet feel hesitantly for the next step.
At last firm ground is reached,
my journey is ended.
I look up: the deep turquoise blue of the sky,
and the silence permeate my being.
I breathe deeply and feel content.

## Gossip

Sometimes they stop at Johnson's to visit,
drink iced tea and pass the time of day,
on snow-white porches lined with red
geranium-filled boxes.
Crimson maple and elm trees parade the streets,
Capped brown roofs, neat sheared lawns
are pleasant parts of small town life.
Gossip comes easily to these visitors,
comfortable with the bits passed on:
Cross, Mrs. Riley's scruffy airdale,
dug up Jones's impatiens bed,
frantic in his search for squirrels;
Young Thomas Moore has run away again.
Will he be found?
Stocks are up, stocks are down,
Battles fought, peace tossed about!
And Miss Nellie Brown, librarian,
has found her love, old William Pierce.

Elizabeth Urquhart

## Mountain Hike

From atop the cold and brilliant peak,
we rest ourselves and wait to speak
of the spectacular view,
the brightness of the day.

We, breathless,
quiet with fast-beating hearts
begin to count the minutes,
when we must depart.

Down we go,
heavy boots grating on the rocks,
holding tight to ropes in steep places,
thanks for the journey of the spirit
shining in our faces.

## Listening

for sounds from the past,
I'm saturated by Irish soft days.
Wind strikes raincoats and I hear
a straight edge slide along my father's
leather strap. In pubs, a pulsing bodhran
is his tapping foot. Sudsy beer drops down
like shaving cream. Once more he sings, *Rings
on her fingers, bells on her toes, elephants
to ride upon my little Irish Rose.* Memories
slide around linoleum, sneak out windows;
sashay through streets.

Shopkeepers, busboys,
musicians, wait to see
if I'll banter with the best.
My flat mid-west accent skips across
their flowing phrases. Laughter ripples.

At restaurants I order salmon knowledge.
Every margin of water calls out verses.
Ogham stones resonate like tuning forks.
Beyond mist elephants trumpet. Rings on
fingers, both shoelaces braided with
bells, I'm ready. My ride waits a few hills
away with an old song.

*Patricia Flower Vermillion*

(b.1932, Akron, Ohio) lives in
Hampton, Virginia. Her words
have appeared in a variety of literary
journals, magazines, and anthologies. She teaches a poetry class in
the school of continuing education
at Christopher Newport
University.

## Voyageur

soil shines
open prairie
does too

blue babe
red rhubarb
lake greens
the shore

always carry
minnesota

*Douglas Alan Wandersee*

grew up in Anoka, Minnesota,
and received his bachelor of arts
in English and psychology from
the University of Minnesota-
Morris in 1993. He moved to the
Shenandoah Valley in 1997 and
received a master of education
from James Madison University
in 1999.

## I Danced at My Daughter's Wedding

In my electric
blue dress

matching shoes
flying

I kissed
all the dragons

and spoke
love words

in their ears.

*Sharon Weinstein*

is a piano teacher, musician, and
artist who resides in Virginia
Beach, Va. Her poems, essays,
and stories have appeared in a
wide range of national publications,
including *Western Humanities Review*,
*Sumi-e National Quarterly*,
*WomenWise*, and *Lilith*. As a pro-
fessor of English and humanities
for many years, she taught at
Arizona State University, Virginia
Wesleyan College, Norfolk State
University, and Hampton University
where she held the endowed chair
of university professor. She gives
creative readings/workshops around
the country, most recently at Sarah
Lawrence College. *Celebrating
Absences* is her first book of poems.

## Life Drawing Class

My sketch pad
balanced on my
thighs

I am moving my
pencil

but it is poems
that are coming

running, spilling
taking shape

on the paper
without me.

Sharon Weinstein

# Grief

It's hard to be angry at a
frail man lying in a thin
shift needles in his arm
his mouth shapeless and
open.

I touched him on
his death-bed more
than I ever touched
him in his whole
life.

On his scratchy cheek
over his wispy hair
holding his hand

I told him:

"You were mean
to me, Dad; you
were mean to all
of us. Someone
should have told
you long ago.

Sorry if I'm
hurting your
feelings."

Part of me feared
his eyes would
blink open and he
would bark at me.

But the rest of me
just loved him.

## Life Lines

I remember a third grade birthday party.
We dressed as gypsies with kerchiefs and
    bracelets.
And delighted in cake and ice cream and prizes.
Off in a corner there was a strange woman
Wearing long skirts and bright dangling earrings.
She sat gazing into a large crystal ball.
Each child, we were told, would have a turn.
To have her very own fortune told.

When my name was called I grew timid, held back;
But she grasped my shy hand and examined
    my palm.
She muttered and mumbled, looked into my eyes.
"I see your fortune, young lady," she said.
    "I see gold. You'll be rich,
    Write books and be praised,
    Gain fame and high office,
    I see power and wealth.
    You will marry a man who
    Who will love you truly.
    You'll have children, be happy
    For many long years."

Much time has elapsed since my fortune was told.
Three score and ten are the years I have seen.
I have written no books nor gained riches and
    praise,
No power nor high office have I ever earned.
But I'm grateful, my darling, for she was
    perceptive.
Even in childhood my life line sought yours.

*Edith R. White*

(b.1923, Passaic, N.J.) storyteller, watercolor painter, and book reviewer; graduated from Vassar College, served two years in Naval Reserve, and is the widow of Dr. Forrest P. White, pediatrician; four children, eight grandchildren, librarian, teacher, lives in Norfolk, Va., enjoys tennis, world travel, painting, and poetry, of course.

Edith R. White

## My Living Trust

My plan is not to spoon mouthfuls of berries
Greedily between crushing teeth,
Taste and juice disappearing in an instant.
Rather take one smooth berry, roll it on my
tongue,
Feel its round blueness, its prickly stem entry,
And savor its smooth, sweet tang.
Then slowly, dreamily, permit its flavor
To seep languidly down my throat.

I want to feel each day round and smooth,
Not crushed and hurried, scooped away in
gluttonous bites,
But made to last as I taste each to the full.
I want to know the earth from which it came,
The seasons turning, sun's warmth, slow
growth,
Sprouting, ripening, sweetening.
When at last it is devoured and gone,
May it linger in memory and flavor my
dreams.

## A New Image

Many years ago I named
The mirror's image "me."
Similar, though not the same,
From was to is—to be?

My mirror, without fail, has shown
A tense, thin lip, an anxious eye;
And we have always known
That mirrors do not lie.

In the mirror of your eye,
A new image of my soul
Gives me back a fuller "I,"
Intact, relaxed, and whole.

Hubert N. Whitten

(b. 1928, Piedmont Plateau, Va.)
graduated from Bridgewater
College and then moved with his
wife to the midwest for 38 years.
Hugh taught high school English
for 25 years in the Elgin, Illinois,
area. In 1988, he and his wife
retired to Bridgewater and now
live in the Bridgewater Retirement
Community. In 2004, Hugh had a
chapbook published, *Piedmont
Poems and Other Reflections*.

## You, Too?

This shy poem hesitates to speak,

Yet, if you say that you, too,
    lie awake at 2:00 a.m. hearing the
    joints crack in a dark house, a dog's
    bark drift over a quiet town, or feel
    life slip away from you like months
    sliding off a calendar.

Or perhaps you also know flashes of joy
    as gathered meanings collect
    like rain puddles in the gutter,
    before they sing down the spout.

If you say these things,
    the poem takes heart,
    its message understood.

## Butterfly

I walk slowly, crawling through my world.
Living my life trying to get from one place to
another.
Wondering why I can't move faster.
Why I can't see more, experience more.

I cannot take it anymore.
Confused, frustrated and depressed.
Why am I here? Why do I exist? What is my
purpose?
Into hiding I go. Retreating into myself.
Wrapping myself in my cocoon.

Then one day, the sun starts to shine on me.
I can see the beautiful sky once again.
I open my wings and fly.
I break out of my cocoon.

I can explore and see the world.
I look at myself and see nothing but beauty.
I am happy, I am free.
I am me.

*Lindsay Williams*

(b.1979, Newport News, Va.)
currently lives in Charlottesville,
Va. She is enrolled part-time in
college and works full time as an
accounts receivables manager for a
publishing company. She began
writing when she was around ten
years old and won an essay contest
at the age of twelve through
WRIC TV 8 in Richmond, Va.
Her college English professor has
used some of her work for his
instruction.

# Take a Look at Your Life

When I was in my forties, a beautiful woman
of 24 fell in love with me.
We worked together and got to know
each other's ways.
She could have had any guy around.
I was married, with three kids
so I don't know why she picked on me

Over a cup of coffee, one morning,
she asked if we could be lovers.
Things weren't going so well at home,
and God, she was gorgeous
but I said no

Later, I thought it over and approached her.
If the offer is still on I say yes,
and so, yes, we became lovers.
Yes, it was like nothing I'd ever known before.
They were writing
good love songs in those days
and I felt like I knew them
from inside out

*I thought our joy would fill the earth
and last til the end of time*

We'd meet at her place,
smoke grass, listen to Roberta Flack
and glorify life

One day, she said we should spend
the rest of our lives together.
I said, *Look, Ellie, I'm an old man
and you are just starting your life.*
She took me in her arms
and made me young once more.

Robert E. Young

(b.1931, Philadelphia, Pa) is a
retired social worker and medical
school professor, living in Virginia
Beach. He was born in Philadelphia
and received a doctorate from the
University of Pennsylvania in
1971. He and his wife enjoy the
ocean and visits with their 5 chil-
dren and 2 grandchildren. His
poems have appeared in the *The
Poet's Domain, Virginia
Adversaria, Powhatan Review,
Chrysler Museum Ekphrasis,
Visions, Nanduti, Pax India,
Voyager,* and *The Open Page.*
Other writings have appeared in
*Port Folio, The Beacon, The Jung
Society Newsletter,* and the Poetry
Society Of Virginia's 80th
Anniversary Anthology.

Robert E. Young

The next day she brought a record
by Neil Young and read the lyrics

*Old man, take a look at my life*
*I'm a lot like you are*

She said, *I've been thinking,*
*we have thirty years. That's all I want.*
I said *no* one more time
and didn't come back.
She went on her way

*Twenty-four and there's so much more*

This afternoon I was driving into Norfolk
and turned the radio on.
The jazz station playing a piano version
of that old Neil Young song.
God, I almost had a wreck.
Been over thirty years.
I'm in my seventies now and take a look at my life.
It's been a good one.
Those few months with her hang 'round

*forever young*


### Passages

Visiting him at college
my son
we went to the courts to play.
For years
we'd been doing the pick and roll
so well at city playgrounds
that few could hang with us.

The kids today are tough
with no respect for elders
and though I loved to rebound,

Robert E. Young

this pimply brat guarding me
was patrolling the boards
like a mean street cat.
I, in my 50s,
could still scratch back.
I snarled.

He gave me a "listen grampaw,
stay in your place."
I, with an urgency
of lifetimes of slights
by nobler men than he,
thrust two lumpy palms into his chest
and barked some school yard at him.

The lad was a tad bigger than I
with nothing yet grown soft.
He did a double-take
as if to say,
"Is it OK
to deck an old man?"

I stood poised—frozen actually—
to take the blow
when Josh,
from two free-throw lanes away
suddenly          star-warred
to a thin space between us,
calmed the assailant
and walked me
into the safety of back court.

My child, father to the man.

## Easter Sunday

For a Jew
to speak at a church on
Easter Sunday, as I did
this morning, is to
resurrect the shadows
of the past, rising up
against them in the
name of faith.

## A Prayer

Rabbi Israel Zoberman

(b.1945, Chu, Kazakhstan,
USSR), ordained as a reform
rabbi by the Hebrew Union
College-Jewish Institute of
Religion in 1974, has been found-
ing rabbi to Congregation Beth
Chaverim in Virginia Beach, Va.,
since 1985. He studied at the
University of Illinois and
McCormick Theological Seminary
(the only rabbi to receive a doctor
of ministry in pastoral care and
counseling from this Presbyterian
institution). His poetry and his
translations from Hebrew have
been published in CCAR Journal,
Poetica, The Jewish Spectator, The
American Rabbi, Moment, and
The Poet's Domain, volumes 5
through 22.

At JFK Airport chapel,
in the guest book,
I found the most
beautiful of prayers.
She wrote, "Here again naturally."

## Only One?

On August 10, a day following the
commemoration of the atomic bomb dropped
on Nagasaki, the elderly Japanese tourist
kept bowing to passengers extending
him courtesies on US Air flight 1598
from Norfolk to Philadelphia.
Was I the only one to notice that he was
a fresh breath of air of an old culture
in the new world?

Rabbi Israel Zoberman

## Last Dance

Determined fallen leaves,
who can stop you?
From a lonely heavenly perch
yearning to join the earth,
unknowingly you plunge
to your death,
but, oh, what a last dance!

## Time

Be kind, life's sculptor,
to the Creator's design,
drawing out what
was intended
to be mine.

## My Kidney Stone

I keep examining with wonder
the kidney stone I just passed,
focusing on its intriguing shape,
as if it were an object
from outer space just concluding
a hazardous journey to Earth.